T0165796

The Spirit of Rome

The Spirit of Rome

Vernon Lee

MINT EDITIONS

The Spirit of Rome was first published in 1910.

This edition published by Mint Editions 2021.

ISBN 9781513295657 | E-ISBN 9781513297156

Published by Mint Editions®

MINT
EDITIONS
minteditionbooks.com

Publishing Director: Jennifer Newens
Design & Production: Rachel Lopez Metzger
Project Manager: Micaela Clark
Typesetting: Westchester Publishing Services

Dis Manibvs Sacrvm.

To All the Friends
Living and Dead
Real and Imaginary
Mortal and Immortal
Who Have Made Rome
What It Is To Me.

Contents

Spring 1899

Explanatory and Apologetic

I was brought up in Rome, from the age of twelve to that of seventeen, but did not return there for many years afterwards. I discovered it anew for myself, while knowing all its sites and its details; discovered, that is to say, its meaning to my thoughts and feelings. Hence, in all my impressions, a mixture of familiarity and of astonishment; a sense, perhaps answering to the reality, that Rome—it sounds a platitude— is utterly different from everything else, and that we are therefore in different relations to it.

Probably for this reason I have found it impossible to use up, in what I have written upon places and their genius, these notes about Rome. I cannot focus Rome into any definite perspective, or see it in the colour of one mood. And whatever may have happened there to my small person has left no trace in what I have written. What I meet in Rome is Rome itself. Rome is alive (only the more so for its occasional air of death), and one is too busy loving, hating, being harassed or soothed, and ruminating over its contradictions, to remember much of the pains and joys which mere mortals have given one in its presence.

A similar reason has prevented all attempt to rewrite or alter these notes. One cannot sit down and attempt a faithful portrait of Rome; at least I cannot. And the value of these notes to those who love Rome, or are capable of loving it, is that they express, in however stammering a manner, what I said to myself about Rome; or, perhaps, if the phrase is not presumptuous, what Rome, day after day and year after year, has said to me.

Autumn, 1903

I

First Return to Rome

Strange that in the confusion of impressions, not new mainly, but oddly revived (the same things transposed by time into new keys), my most vivid impression should be of something so impersonal, so unimportant, as an antique sarcophagus serving as base to a mediæval tomb. Impressions? Scarcely. My mind seems like an old blotting-book, full of fragments of sentences, of words suggesting something, which refuses to absorb any more ink.

How I had forgotten them, and how well I know them, these little details out of the past! The darkish sponge-like holes in the travertine, the reversed capital on the Trinità dei Monti steps, the caryatides of the Stanza dell' Incendio, the scowl or smirk of the Emperors and philosophers at the Capitol: a hundred details. I seem to have been looking at nothing else these fifteen years, during which they have all been absolutely forgotten.

The very Campagna today, driving out beyond Cecilia Metella, little as I knew it before, seems quite familiar, leaves no impression. Yes, the fences tied like that with reeds, overtopped by sprouting elders, the fat weeds on wall and tomb, the undulations of sere green plain, the white snow-masses floating, as it were, in the blue of the sky; the straddling bits of aqueduct, the lumps of masonry. Am I utterly and for ever spoilt for this? Has it given me so much that it can never give me any more?— that the sight of Arezzo and its towers beneath the blueness and the snow of Falterona, the green marshy valley, with the full Tiber issuing from beneath the last Umbrian Mountains, seemed so much more poignant than all this. Is it possible that Rome in three days can give me nothing more vivid and heady than the thought of that sarcophagus, let into the wall of the Ara Coeli, its satyrs and cupids and grapes and peacocks surmounted by the mosaic crosses, the mediæval inscriptions of Dominus Pandulphus Sabelli?

Rome, *February* 1888

II

A Pontifical Mass at the Sixtine Chapel

I never knew so many hours pass so pleasantly as in this tribune, surrounded by those whispering, elbowing, plunging, veiled women in black, under the wall painted with Perugino's Charge of St. Peter, and dadoed with imitation Spanish leather, superb gold and blue scrolls of Rhodian pomegranate pattern and Della Rovere shields with the oak-tree.

My first impression is of the magnificence of all these costumes, the Swiss with their halberts, the Knights of Malta, the Chamberlains like so many Rubenses or Frans Halses, the Prelates and cardinals, each with his little train of purple priestlets; particularly of the perfection in wearing these clothes, something analogous to the brownish depth of the purple, the carnation vividness of the scarlet, due to all these centuries of tradition. At the same time, an impression of the utter disconnectedness of it all, the absence of all spirit or meaning; this magnificence being as the turning out of a great rag bag of purple and crimson and gold, of superb artistic things all out of place, useless, patternless, and almost odious: pageantry, ritual, complicated Palestrina music, crowded Renaissance frescoes, that huge Last Judgment, that mass of carefully grouped hideous nudities, brutal, butcher-like, on its harsh blue ground; that ceiling packed with superb pictures and figures, symmetrical yet at random, portentous arm and thighs and shoulders hitting one as it were in the eye. The papal procession, white robes, gold candlesticks, a wizen old priest swaying, all pale with sea-sickness, above the crowd, above the halberts and plumes, between the white ostrich fans, and dabbing about benedictions to the right and left. The shuffle of the people down onto their knees, and scuffle again onto their feet, the shrill reading of the Mass, and endless unfinished cadences, overtopped by unearthly slightly sickening quaverings of the choir; the ceaseless moving about of all this mass of black backs, veils, cloaks, outlines of cheek and ear presenting every now and then among the various kinds of rusty black; no devotion, no gravity, no quiet anywhere, among these creatures munching chocolates and adjusting opera-glasses. M.P's voice at my ear, now about Longus and Bonghi's paganism, now about the odiousness of her neighbour who won't let her climb on her seat, the dreadful grief of not seeing the Cardinal's tails, the wonderfulness of Christianity having come out of people like the Apostles (I having turned out Gethsemane in St. Matthew in the Gospel which she brought, together with a large supply of chocolate and the Fioretti di S. Francesco), the ugliness of the women, &c. &c. And meanwhile the fat pink profile perdu, the *toupé* of grey hair like powder of a colossal soprano sways to and fro fatuously over the gold grating above us.

All this vaguely on for a space of time seeming quite indeterminate. Little by little, however, a change came over things, or my impression of them. Is it that one's body being well broken, one's mind becomes more susceptible of homogeneous impressions? I know not. But the higher light, the incense, fills the space above all those black women's heads, over the tapers burning yellow on the carved marble balustrades with the Rovere arms, with a luminous grey vagueness; the blue background of the *Last Judgment* grows into a kind of deep hyacinthine evening sky, on which twist and writhe like fleshy snakes the group of demons and damned, the naked Christ thundering with His empty hand among them; the voices moving up and down, round and round in endless unended cadences, become strange instruments (all sense of register and vocal cords departing), unearthly harps and bugles and double basses, rasping often and groaning like a broken-down organ, above which warbles the hautboy quaver of the sopranos. And the huge things on the ceiling, with their prodigious thighs and toes and arms and jowls crouch and cower and scowl, and hang uneasily on arches, and strain themselves wearily on brackets, dreary, magnificent, full of inexplicable feelings all about nothing: the colossal prophetic creature in green and white over the altar, on the keystone of the vault, striking out his arms— to pull it all down or prop it all up? The very creation of the world becoming the creation of chaos, the Creator scudding away before Himself as He separates the light from the darkness. Chaos, chaos, and all these things moving, writhing, making fearful efforts, in a way living, all about nothing and in nothing, much like those voices grating and quavering endlessly long.

ROME, *March* 4, 1888

III

Second Return to Rome

I feel very much the grandeur of Rome; not in the sense of the heroic or tragic; but grandeur in the sense of splendid rhetoric. The great size of most things, the huge pilasters and columns of churches, the huge stretches of palace, the profusion of water, the stature of the people, their great beards and heads of hair, their lazy drawl—all this tends to the grand, the emphatic. It is not a grandeur of effort and far-fetchedness like that of Jesuit Spain, still less of achievement and restrained force like that of Tuscany. It is a splendid wide-mouthed rhetoric; with a meaning certainly, but with no restriction of things to mere meaning.

The man who has understood Rome best, in this respect, is Piranesi. His edifices, always immensely too big, his vegetation, extravagantly too luxurious, are none too much to render Rome. And those pools of blackness and immense lakes of ink.

Rome, *February* 20, 1889

IV

Ara Coeli

Ended the morning characteristically at Ara Coeli, one of the churches here I like best, or rather one of the few I like at all. I find that the pleasure I derive from churches is mainly due to their being the most *inhabited* things in the world: inhabited by generation after generation, each bringing its something grand or paltry like its feelings, sometimes things stolen from previous generations like the rites themselves with their Pagan and Hebrew colour; bringing something, sticking in something, regardless of crowding (as life is ever regardless of other life): tombs, pictures, silver hearts and votive pictures of accidents and illnesses, paper flowers, marbled woodwork pews, hangings. And each generation also wearing something away, the bricks and marble discs into unevenness, the columns into polish, effacing with their tread the egotism of the effigies, reducing them to that mere film, mere outline of rigid feet, cushioned head and folded hands which is so pious and pathetic.

Such a church as Ara Coeli—like those of Ravenna—has this character all the more, that its very pillars are stolen from antique edifices, and show, in their broken flutings or scarred granite, that the weather also has felt its feelings about them, that they have shared in the life not merely of this religion or of that, Pagan or Christian, but in the life of the winds and rains. Such churches as this, anything but swept and garnished, correspond in a way to Browning's poetry; there is the high solemnity brought home to you, not disturbed, by the very triviality of the details; mysteries and wonders overarching the real living life of ex-votos and pictures of runaway horses and houses on fire; the life worn like the porphyry discs of the pavement, precious bits trodden into the bricks, the life of the present filched out of the past, like the columns of the temple supporting arches painted with seventeenth-century saints.

The organ was playing to the chanting of the monks; and standing before the chapel of S. Bernardino, where the Christ in the gold almond and the worshipping and music-making angels of Pinturicchio rise out of the blue darkness behind the grating, I felt oddly that music of the organ. The sonorous rasping of the bass tubes, the somewhat nasal quaver of the vox humana and the hautboy, was actually the music made by these beribboned Umbrian angels, those long ages ago, in the gloom of their blue cloudy sky, with the blessing, newly arisen Christ in the cherub-spangled gold almond among them.

Holy Saturday

V

Villa Cæsia

Several miles along the Via Nomentana, we came to a strange place, situate in an oasis in the wilderness, or rather in what is already the beginning of a new country—the mere mounds of tufo turning into high slopes, and a few trees (it is odd how they immediately give a soul to this soulless desert), leafless at present, serpentine along the greener grass. And there, with the russet of an oakwood behind, rises a square huddle of buildings, a tall brick watch-tower, battlemented and corbelled in the midst, and a great bay-tree at each corner. On the tower, immediately below the battlements, is the inscription, in huge letters, made, I should think, of white majolica tiles—Villa Cæsia. The lettering, besides being broken, is certainly not modern, and has a sharpness of outline telling of the Renaissance.

What solitary humanist may have put up that inscription, coming out from Rome to commune in that wilderness, amid the rustle of the oakwood and of the laurel-trees, and the screaming of magpies and owls, with the togaed poets and philosophers of the Past?

VI

The Pantheon

The back of the Pantheon, and its side, as seen from the steps of the Minerva, the splendid circle of masonry, and arched courses of rose-coloured brickwork, lichened and silvered over, broken off, turned into something almost like a natural cliff of rosy limestone; and at its foot the capitols of magnificent columns, and fragments of delicate dolphined frieze.

VII

By the Cemetery

I am struck again this time by one of the things which on my first return after so many years got to mean for my mind Rome. The Aventine, where it slopes down to the Tiber white with fruit blossom, the trees growing freely in masonry and weeds, against the moist sky; this ephemeral exquisiteness seeming to mean more here among the centuries than in any other place.

I was right, I think, when I wrote the other day that it would be easier for us to face the thought of danger, death, change, here in Rome than elsewhere. K. told me she felt it when we met at the Cemetery at her poor old aunt's grave. To die here might seem, one would think, more like re-entering into the world's outer existence, returning, as Epictetus has it, *where one is wanted*. The cypresses of the graveyard, there under the city walls, among the ruins, do not seem to unite folk with the terrible unity Death, so much as with the everlasting life of the centuries.

March 4, 1893

SPRING 1895

I

Villa Livia

Along the road to Civita Castellana, absolutely deserted. The Tiber between low, interrupted slopes, some covered with longest most compact green grass, others of brown, unreal tufo, like crumbled masonry, or hollowed into Signorelli-looking grottoes, with deep growths of Judas-tree, broom, and scant asphodels; all green and brown, of such shapes that one wonders whether they also, like so many seeming boulders scattered in their neighbourhood, are not in reality masonry, long destroyed towns.

The Tiber, pale fawn colour, flush, among greenness, receiving delicate little confluents which have come along under lush foliage; smooth dark shallow streams, stoneless on sandy bottom; one imagines each fought about in those first Roman days. The country is a great pale circular greenness under tender melting sky, with pale distant mountains all round.

How Rome seems to have been isolated from all life save the life eternal and unchangeable of grass and water, and cattle and larks; to have been suspended in a sort of void!

Further along, reed hovels (some propped in aqueduct arches), hovels also in caves, and squalid osterias, into whose side are built escutcheoned mediæval capitals. A few mounted drovers trot slowly by.

At Prima Porta, in this wilderness, a hillock of grass, descending into which you find a small chamber painted all round with a deep hedge of orchard and woodland plants, pomegranates, apples, arbutus, small pines and spruce firs, all most lovingly and knowingly given, with birds nesting and pecking, in brilliant enamel like encaustic on an enamel blue sky.

Coming home in rain, Rome appears with cupola of St. Peter's and Vatican gardens so disposed as to seem only a colossal sanctuary in the wilderness.

May 8

II

Colonna Gallery

Durer?? Portrait of a red-haired Colonna with the ruins of Rome behind him; ruins which, with his violent, wild-man-of-the-woods face, he looks as if he had made.

III

San Saba

The lovely floor, the minute pieces of marble forming a far-more-lovely-than possible faded purple and lilac rug. Also, the pathetically trodden-down-to-bits porphyry discs in the doorway. And the little cippus of a Roman girl who lived sixteen years and twenty-eight days. Against the apse, outside, the great python of a cactus.

Looking down into the deserted church through the window of the loggia, one half expects to see stoled ghosts in the vagueness below. Outside and opposite, the immense counterforts of the Palatine, and its terrace and sparse cypresses.

IV

S. Paolo Fuori

The wonderful loveliness of the double colonnade of polished granite pillars on the polished pale grey marble floor; fantastic, like transfigured pools and streams of purest water.

May 9

V

PINETA TORLONIA

Asphodels on the banks. As we come up, the peasants drive into the stable, one by one, a lot of mares with their foals. Along the road a drove of great long-horned grey oxen; a bull-calf canters among them. Between us and St. Peter's is a dell full of scrub ilex; walls also, full of valerian and that grey myrrh-like weed.

From that little height we face a tremendous black storm, against which all the Sabine and Alban hills flash in the low sunlight, above the green Campagna pale like a strip of sea.

May 12

SPRING 1897

I

Return at Midnight

Driving from the station at midnight, the immensity of everything, gigantic proportions of silent palaces and closed churches. Passing in front of the Quirinal, the colossal Dioscuri with their horses, the fountain flowing down and spurting upwards between them, white under the electric light, against the deep blue darkness.

Even the incredible huge vulgarity of modern things, advertisements, yards long at the street corners under the gas, and immense rows of jerry-built houses, somehow help to make up the impression of Rome as a theatre of the ages: a gigantic stage, splendidly impressive to eye and fancy, where Time has strutted and ranted, and ever will continue.

At night particularly one feels the Piranesi grandeur, but also the Callot picturesqueness which are secondary qualities of Rome. As a whole the town belongs mainly to the shabby and magnificent seventeenth century. Those hundreds of architecturally worthless Jesuit churches are not, as we are apt stupidly to say, absurd or meaningless, but quite the contrary; admirably suited to their place and function among ruins and vagueness. The beggars and loafers, the inconceivable squalor and lousiness, are also, in this sense, in their rights.

March 24

II

Villa Madama

The great empty, unfinished, hulk, very grand and with delicate details, stranded like the ark on Ararat on its hillside of brushwood and market-garden, seems to sum up, in a shape only a little more splendid than usual, the story told on all sides. For on all sides there are great mouldering unfinished villas, barrocco casinos, even fifteenth-century small palaces, deserted among the fields; and everywhere monumental gateways leading to nothing. Their story is that of the unceasing enterprise of pope after pope, and cardinal after cardinal against the inexorable climate of Rome. Each shortlived generation of old men, come to Rome too late to learn, already accustomed to order about and to swagger, refusing to see the ruins left by its predecessors; insisting on having its way with those malarious hillocks and riversides; only to die like the rest, leaving another gaunt enclosure behind.

One of the fascinations of Rome is undoubtedly not its murderous quality as such, but the character of which that seems a part, the quality of being a living creature, with unbreakable habits and unanswerable reasons, making it massacre quite quietly, whatever came in its way.

Rome, as perhaps only Venice, is an organic city, almost a living being; its *genius loci* no allegory, but its own real self.

March

VERNON LEE

III

From Valmontone to Olevano

Valmontone, on the railway line to Naples, to which we bicycled back from Segni—a savage village on a hill, pigs burrowing and fighting at its foot—and on its skirt a great stained Palazzo Farnese-like palace.

Crossing the low hills of the wide valley between the Alban and Sabine chains, magnificent bare mountains appear seated opposite, crystalline, almost gemlike; and splendid, almost crepuscular, colours in the valley even at noon: deep greens and purples, the pointed straw stacks replacing, as black accents, our Tuscan cypresses. Quantities of blue and white wind-flowers on the banks, and wine-coloured anemones under the thick ilex-like olives; and all round the splendid pale-blue chains of jagged and conical mountains. A population of tattered people and galled horses; much misery; a sort of more savage Umbrian landscape, and without Umbrian serenity; deserted, deserted roads. I am writing from the olive yard above the inn; the rugged little Olevano hanging, almost sliding, down the hillside opposite, black houses and yellow-lichened roofs.

OLEVANO, *March* 28

IV

From Olevano to Subiaco

Yesterday afternoon bicycled and walked from Olevano to Subiaco. A steep mile and a half up to the very crest of the mountains, and then down some sharp corners and one or two very precipitous zigzags, letting myself run down; the first time I have had such a sensation, a sensation largely of fear, partly of joy: a changing view in front, on the side—steeps of sere woods, great mountains, like jasper or some other stone that should be veined amethyst, a smell of freshness, whiffs of violets, at one point a small green lake deep, deep below (Stagno di Rojate); yet an annihilation of both space and time. It was better when Ch. Br. and I dismounted and walked down; the road cut out of the steep wooded hills; on the shady side trickling with water and delicious with moss, primroses, and violets among the sere chestnuts. Here and there a cherry-tree in the valley deep below, like a little puff of smoke. The sweetness of those mountain woods with the great bare lilac mountains all round!

A sharp zigzag, a swish over a bridge, where as one rather felt than saw the full green Anio dashing through rocks; and just at sunset we came upon Subiaco—rising violet, with its great pointing castle mound, from the green valley of water and budding poplars into a purple and fiery sky. Then in the dusk through the little town, where the bells were ringing.

Tivoli, *March* 29

V

Acqua Marcia

I sha'n't forget, on the long bleak road from Subiaco to Vicovaro, a violent dry wind against us, veiling all things in dust, a spring near Spiagge: a wide runnel of water spirting out of the travertine and running off into clear rills where the mules drink. The water they collect up here for the Acqua Marcia, whose aqueducts we see about, old arches and new; water, cold, infinitely pure, exquisite, one might say almost fragrant. It was such spirts from the rock, as well as the sight of pure mountain streams, which taught St. Francis his verse about Suor Acqua. St. Francis must have wandered in these fastnesses which (totally unlike the country between Segni and Olevano) are very Umbrian in character. There is a portrait of him, said to be by a contemporary monk, on a pilaster of one of the subterranean chapels of the Sacro Speco above Subiaco: blond, wide-eyed, the cowl drawn over his head.

Tivoli, *March* 29

VI

The Sacro Speco

The Sacro Speco was a very charming surprise. The series of little churches and chapels up and down flights of steps, vaulted and painted in Gothic style, with shrine lamps here and there, were quite open and empty. We walked into them, or rather into a crooked vestibule frescoed by some Umbrian, with no sudden transition from the splendid grove of ilexes, immense branches like beams overhead, from the great hillside of bluish-grey tufo, with only a few bitter herbs on it. The convent of the Sacro Speco is a half-fortified little place into which we could not penetrate. Only a surly monk, found with difficulty (another entered the chapels with a great bundle of wall-flowers and irises), took us into the microscopic garden under the convent battlements hedged with flowering rosemary, where the roses in which St. Benedict rolled are grown (May roses, only bright leaves as yet) literally in the shape of a bed or gridiron, row along row.

Though it is not remote-looking, 'tis a splendid place for a hermit's thoughts: the blue-grey hillside running down into the green rushing Anio, the great bare bluish mountains all round, far enough to be visible, a great sense of air and space, for a valley. No vegetation, save a few olives and scrub oaks and the bitter herbs and euphorbus. No scented happy Tuscan things. And deep below, the arches of Nero's Villa—with demons no doubt galore. Those giottesque chapels hold in them, all hung with lamps, a small tufo grotto, the one down which, as in Sodoma's fresco, the angels sent baskets of provisions and the devils made horns at St. Benedict.

Rome, *March* 30

VII

The Valley of the Anio

There is a nice Cosmati cloister at S. Scolastica, lower on the hill, an enormous also fortified-looking monastery, but to which also there is only a mule path. These places are splendidly *meditative*, but they do not give me the idea of hermitages in the wilderness like that ruined Abbey of Sassovivo above Foligno. But the Sacro Speco's little up and down chapels, a miniature Assisi, empty, yet not abandoned on this sunburnt rock, are very impressive.

I take great pleasure following the Anio, which we first met coming out of the narrow gorge round the S. Scolastica hill (the other side behind Nero's ruins is a hill covered with pale green scrub, beech, or more likely alder), down below Subiaco. In the ever-widening valley it is an impetuous stream, but not at all a torrent; pale green filling up a narrow bed between pale green willows, here and there slackening into pools with delicate green waving plants: a very unexpected and (to me) inexplicable sight among those mountains which are more arid than any Tuscan ones, and from which very few tributary streams seem to descend. (I can remember crossing only one, full and with waving weeds also.)

The Anio swirls round a beautiful wooded promontory, ilexes and even a few cypresses, between Spiagge and Vicovaro, making a little church into a miniature Tivoli Sibilla. One becomes very fond of such a stream, and it is a great delight to see it in its triumph at Tivoli racing headlong into the abyss of the big fall, only a spray cloud revealing it among the thick green; or breaking out into tiny delicate fountains—garden fountains, you would think—among the ilexes and grottoes under the little round Temple; a wonderful mixture of wildness and art, a place, with its high air, its leaping waters and glimpses of distant plain, such as one would really wish for a sibyl, and might imagine for Delphi. An enchanted place with its flight and twitter of birds above the water. I should like to follow the Anio into the Tiber.

At sunset, had there been one, we went into the Villa d'Este, entering through the huge deserted courts and grottoed halls of the colossal palace, surprised to find the enchanted gardens, the terraces and cypresses descending on the other side, the grey vague plain and distant mountains—and always the sound of waters. What a solemn magnificent place! How strange a contrast from the Benedictine monastery on its arid rocks, to this huge, solemn, pompous palace, with its plumed gardens and statued hedges, hanging on a hillside too, but what a different one!

Rome, *March* 30

VIII

VICOVARO

There was cultivation all down the valley of the Anio, lots of blossoming cherry-trees; and the peasant-women in stays, and some men in knee breeches, looked prosperous. Subiaco seeming a sort of S. Marcello.

Vicovaro is a delightful village above the Anio, with a fine palace of the Bolognettis, a good many houses with handsome carved windows and lintels as in Umbria, a nice circular church with fourteenth-century elaborate statued porch, and a very charming temple portico. Here also the people looked well-to-do and civilised, on the whole like Umbrians; whereas on the Olevano side, even on Sunday, they were in rags and miserably stolid. The little caffè where we eat was lined with political caricatures.

Places like Vicovaro and still more the many apparently inaccessible other villages incredibly high up—Cantalupo, Castel Madama, S. Vito, &c., each with its distinguishing *palazzone*—makes one understand *what Rome is made of*—the feudal, savage mountains whence, even like its drinking water which splashes in Bernini fountains, this sixteenth and seventeenth century Rome has descended. *For Rome is not an Urban City*; and underneath all the Bernini palaces, we must imagine things like Palazzo Capranica, with the few mullioned and Gothic windows picked in its fortress-like walls. How I seem to feel what Rome is made of—its strange living components in the past!

At Subiaco the streets were strewn, as for a procession, with shredded petals of violets. All kinds of violets grow on those hills, some reddish and as big as pansies; and as we swished past, instead of the dry scent of myrrh and mint of our Tuscan hills, there came a moist smell of violets from the hedgerows.

ROME, *March* 31

IX

Tor Pignattara

Drove today with Maria outside Porta Maggiore, little changed since my childhood. Stormy sunshine, the mountains blue, with patches of violet, like dark rainbow splendours, flashing out with white towns; cherry blossoms among the reeds, vague gardens with statues and bits of relief stuck about. Finally the circular domed tomb of Empress Helena, with a tiny church, a bit of orphanage built into it, and all round the priest's well-kept garden and orphans' vegetable garden. A sound of harmonium and girls' hymn issuing out of the ruin, on which grow against the sky great tufts of fennel, of stuff like London pride and of budding lentisk. This *is* Rome!

March 31

X

Villa Adriana

We crossed the Anio twice—first at Ponte Mammolo, where it is Tiber-coloured, and it tugs at the willows; then before it has been polluted by the sulphur water of the Acque Albule (though the sulphur blue water is itself lovely) at a magnificent tower under Tivoli, like Cecilia Metella. An Anio green, rushing flush as at Subiaco, among poplars and willows, fields of sprouting reeds.

Villa Adriana: you see it from a distance at the foot of the Tivoli hills—sloping olive woods and domes of pines. What a place! The Armida gardens for a Faust-Rinaldo. Antiquity like a *belle au bois dormant* in the groves of colossal ilexes, the rows of immense cypresses, above all, enclosed in the magic of those thick old silver-coloured huge unpruned olives, of the high flowering grasses. These vestiges of porticoes and domes and grottoes are not in the least beautiful architecturally; and every statue, every bit of frieze has been ruthlessly removed, only the broken slabs of marble, of wainscot and a few broken mosaics remaining—'tis the only garden near Rome with not *one* statue in it! But somehow the divine vegetation, the divine view of near blue mountains and blue plain seem to transform all this brick and cement into something beautiful and precious, to turn the few remaining columns and stalked broken capitals (all the rest, vases, baths, floors, marbles, gone to the Vatican) into something exquisite. Perhaps 'tis the very absence of statues which makes one think what statues must have stood there, and feel as if they were still present. Anyhow this quite accidental place, this vanished palace covered over by the olive groves, the box hedges, cypress avenues and pastures of little trumpery farm villas—is far more beautiful and wonderful than any of the art-made Roman gardens, and is, so to speak, their *original*—much as those Tivoli falls seem the prototype of all the Roman fountains.

It began to rain as we were there, and thundered through the great halls. Then as it cleared over the mountains, the plain green, vague! was blotted with black rain, a threatening yellow sky above.

April 10

XI

S. Lorenzo Fuori

The fine *ambones*; the very peculiar and beautiful galleries, with delicate columns, like a triforium on either side of choir for women; the choir with splendid episcopal seat and pale cipolin benches—Tadema like—for priests all round.

We must imagine classic antiquity full of this wonderful blond colour of marbles; arrangements of palest lilac, green, rosy yellow, and a white shimmer. Colours such as we see on water at sunset, ineffable.

April 10

XII

On the Alban Hills

The big olives, pruned square, but of full dense foliage, not smoke-like, but the colour of old dark silver; the vineyards of pale criss-cross blond canes on violet ground. The railway goes round Lake Albano, reflecting blue stormy sky and white cloud balls; a gash when the current alters shows marvellous hyacinth blue. A fringe of budding little trees and of great pale asphodels; the smell of them and of freshness.

Beautiful circular church, cupola silvery, ribbed outside, at Ariccia, opposite Palazzo Chigi; a great grim palace, stained grey with damp and time, flanked by four sorts of towers; windows scarce. This solemn type of sixteenth-century *White Devil of Italy* palace or villa recurs in this neighbourhood; places to keep their secrets; some apparently on the very border of the Campagna, where vines and olives end. Wonderful woods full of flowers between Albano and Genzano.

The little round Lake of Nemi disappointed me.

Bicycling to Marino, Lake Albano seen from above, waters reflecting black storm, sere oakwoods of Rocca di Papa stormy purple too, and round the highest Latin peak, which looks like an altar slab, a great inky storm, water, hills, sky, all threatening inky green and violet; and against them, on the hill ridge of stones, the delicate pale pink chandeliers of the asphodels.

On the other side the slopes of vineyards and pale blue campagna and faint shining sea line, blond under a clear sky. Lovely woods of oak near Marino, through which, alas! we swished down hill. A whole flock of sheep, newly raddled, and faunlike shepherds lying in the shade opposite.

In Villa Torlonia at Albano, a pond, surrounded by masks (whence water spouted), deep green water, broken by fountain, green deep ilex groves round; every stone picked out with delicate green moss. And at the end of the vistas the campagna in green, purple blue modelling of evening, hillocks and farms and aqueducts, hay and straw stacks vaguely visible. And beyond the white shiny sea. The storm has disappeared, leaving only a few clouds veiling the Subiaco mountains which we see. How different in memory from these Latin Hills! All up the hill great terraced gardens, piled-up villas: Aldobrandini, Falconieri, Lancillotti.

ROME, *April* 13

XIII

Maundy Thursday

Yesterday, Giovedi Santo evening, the washing of the high-altar of St. Peter's. A sudden impression of the magnificence of this church, its vastness filled with dusk, a few wax tapers scattered along the nave; in the far distance a lit-up altar throwing its light up into the vault of an aisle, showing the shimmer of golden coffering; the crowd circling unseen.

Then the ceremony of washing the high-altar: all the canons, priests and choir-boys mounted onto its dais; and, as they passed, wiped the great slab with a brush of white shavings dipped in oil and wine; then walked round the church in solemn procession, tiny choir-boys first, purple canons, and, lastly, a tall cardinal with scarlet cap, all with their white mops; a penetrating sweet smell of wine and oil filling the place, and seeming to waken paganism. As they turned again towards the high-altar, its huge twisted gilded columns glimmering in the light of the tapers, lights appeared in the Veronica balcony; priests moved to and fro with a great gold cross in that distant lit-up gloom; the canons fell on their knees, great purple poppies. There was the noise of a rattle; more lights in that balcony, and another gold shining thing was displayed; the Veronica this time, with (as you guessed) the outline of a bearded face.

It was twilight outside; and St. Peter's, its colonnade, St. Angelo's, the Tiber, looked colossal.

Maundy Thursday

XIV

GOOD FRIDAY

It was overcast yesterday, and the sun set as we approached this place, the train passing through woods of myrtle and lentisk scrub. Suddenly we came upon green fields lying against the skyline, and full of asphodels—a pale golden-rosy sunset under mists, a pinkish full moon rising in the misty blue opposite; and against this pale, serene sky, the hundreds of asphodels, each distinct like a candlestick, rising out of the green. I never saw such a vision of the Elysian fields.

Here at Anzio we found a Gesù Morto procession winding with a band, and a red-and-white confraternity, through the little fishing town. At one moment the great black erect Madonna appeared among the torch-light against the deep blue sky, the misty blue moonlit sea.

Much less fine than such processions are in Tuscany; but impressive. The little boats, with folded lateen sails, near the pier had coloured lanterns slung from the mast to the bowsprit. The sea broke like ruffled silk.

ANZIO, *April* 17

XV

ASPHODELS

Like Johnson and his wall-fruit, I have never had as many asphodels to look at as I wanted. Ever since I saw them first, rushing by train through the Maremma, nay ever since I saw them in a photograph of a Sicilian temple, nay perhaps, secretly, since hearing their name, I have felt a longing for them, and a secret sense that I was never going to be shown as many as I want. Here I have. Yesterday morning bicycling inland, along a rising road along which alternate green pastures and sea, and woods of dense myrtle and lentisk scrub overtopped by ilexes and cork-trees, *there were asphodels enough*: deep plantations, little fields, like those of cultivated narcissus, compact masses of their pale salmon and grey shot colours and greyish-green leaves, or fringes, each flower distinct against field or sky, on the ledges of rock and the high earth banks. The flowers are rarely perfect when you pick them, some of the starry blossoms having withered and left an untidy fringe instead; but at a distance this half-decay gives them a singular distinction, makes the light fall on the very tips, the silvery buds, sinking the stretching out branches and picking out the pale rose colour with grey. The beauty of the plant is in the candlestick thrust of the branches. The flower has a faint oniony smell, but fresh like box hedge.

ANZIO, EASTER DAY

XVI

Nettuno

Nettuno, a little castellated town on the rocks; battlemented walls and towers, a house with fortified windows, a sixteenth-century fortress, very beautiful. All manner of vines, weeds and lilac flowers growing in the walls. Men in boots and breeches and brigand hats about, women with outside stays. In the evening a flock of goats being milked. Strings of mules, literally strings, beasts tied together.

Last evening we bicycled beyond Nettuno on the way to Torre Astura, which you see bounding this semicircular gulf, vague great mountains behind. The Cape of Circe, which looks (and surely must have been) an island, came out faint towards evening, a great cliff ending in something like a castle, apparently in the middle of the sea, mysterious. We got, skirting the sea, to a large heath—a heath, black sandy soil, of budding bracken, grass and asphodels; immense, inexpressibly solemn and fresh; a little wood of cork-trees in the distance, a broken Roman ruin, blue Apennines half hidden in clouds. A few shepherds were going home, looking immense on the flatness, and goats and horses. Song of larks, and suddenly an unexpected booming of surf. Following the sound inexplicably loud, across the deeper black sandy soil, we got to the sea. Most strange against it, a fringe of marshy grass, of bulrushes! Far off the tower of Astura, and the faint Cape of Circe among mists. It began to rain.

Anzio, *Easter*

XVII

Torre Astura

Yesterday evening bicycled farther in the direction of Torre Astura, which seemed quite near in its solitude. The dunes were covered with thick bushes of lentisk, myrtle and similar shrubs; every step bruised some scented thing. Along the sands, black, hard and full of coloured shells, was a strip of bulrushes. The sea, which is tame and messy in the artificial bay formed by the pier of Anzio, was fresh and rushing; the wind swept the brown dark sand like smoke along the ground.

Monte Circeo was quite distinct, blue and white its summit an overhanging rock, no castle. Inland stretched the fields of asphodels and the deep woods.

We found in the morning a lane or road gone to ruin, running high up from Anzio to Nettuno, and entirely under splendid overarching ilexes; a sunk lane, with here and there a glimpse of blue sea among the evergreen branches.

Anzio, *April* 19

SPRING 1899

I

The Walls

Drove from Porta Angelica to Porta Portese; an immense round, possible, conceivable, only in Rome. I see for the first time the *outside* of the Vatican, galleries and gardens, realising the sort of fortified town it is, a Rome within Rome. And a fortified one: that long passage (Hall of the Ariadne) between the Belvedere and the Rotunda has battlements (oddly enough, Ghibelline); there are towers and counterforts I cannot identify; and then the immense buttressed walls, with their green vegetation, and slabs and coats of arms of Medicis, Roveres; with the clipped ilexes of the gardens, the pines and bays overtopping, on and on. And in a gap, suddenly, and close enough to take one's breath away, the immensity of St. Peter's and the Cupola.

And that this town, which is the Vatican and St. Peter's, these centres of so much life, should, as a fact, look on one side straight onto forsaken roads, and the most desolate of countries! Such a thing is impossible except in Rome; and even in Rome I never suspected it.

Continuing outside the walls, we come to the little church of San Pancrazio, on an empty road hedged with reed-tied dry thorns: the little porched doorway leading into an atrium which is an olive garden, big old trees set orderly, and a pillar with the cross; outside at least, a solemn little basilica, making one think of Ravenna.

We drove, apparently for miles, up and down, round and round, between two immediately successive gates, San Pancrazio and Portese. Green slopes, dry vineyards with almond blossom among the criss-cross canes, brakes of reeds; here and there rows of little triumphal bay-trees in flower over the walls; great overhanging ornamental gateways, leading to nothing; and, at long intervals, mouldering little villas and *trattorie*, with mulberry-trees clipped into umbrellas. Rome totally disappeared, hidden, heaven knows where, in this country of which there seems an unlimited amount: always more green slopes, more dry vineyards, more distant Campagna. And yet, seemingly close by, the great bells of St. Peter's ring out the thanksgiving service for the Pope.

Antonia said, "Shall we go for a minute into St. Peter's? It will be all lit up."

And, in that endless emptiness, the words sounded absurd. St. Peter's? Rome? Where?

March 13

II

Palazzo Cenci

This morning, rambling along the unfinished Tiber quays, and the half pulled-down houses of the old Jewish quarter, attracted a little, perhaps, by the name "Vicolo dei Cenci," I let myself be importuned by a red-haired woman into entering the Casa di Beatrice Cenci, a dreary, squalid palace, given over to plasterers among the dust-heaps.

And afterwards, beguiled further up flights and flights of black stairs into someone's filthy little kitchen, I was made to look down, through a mysterious window, into the closed church of the Cencis. Looking down, always a curious impression, into a dark, musty place and onto vague somethings which are, they tell me, the tombs of the Cencis.

A grim and sordid impression altogether; and heaven knows how sickening a story. Yet what power of popular romance, of great poetry, has enveloped it all! A story one would be ashamed to read through in a cheap newspaper. . . and yet! . . .

March 24

III

Monte Cavo

Yesterday, with Maria, Antonia, and the poet Pascarella, to Rocca di Papa, lunching in a piece of the woods which M. has bought.

The grass of the campagna, beyond the aqueducts, is powdered with daisies like a cake with sugar. Further, where the slopes begin, the exquisite brilliant pink of the peach blossom is on the palest yellow criss-cross of reeds in the dry vineyards.

I am struck once more by the majestic air of that opening square of Frascati, expanding upwards into terraces, lawns, and ilexes, all flanked by pinnacled and voluted buildings, Villa Aldobrandini, or whatever it is.

We drive up through the sere chestnut woods, where wind-flowers and blue squills come up everywhere among the russet leaves. Suddenly, in the faint light, above a clearing, the stacked white trunks, the lilac sereness of the trees; and high up, shimmering and misty, the rock of Rocca di Papa with its piled-up houses.

Then through the woods again, on foot, up a path first deep in dry leaves, then paved with hard volcanic flags; chestnut woods, but no longer cut for charcoal (the smoke of its burning rises from below), but in clumps, straight slender boles rising from immense roots. Chestnuts so unlike those of our Apennines that, when, higher up, they are exchanged for beeches, it is only by picking up the fallen dry leaves that we could tell the difference. And beyond, descending towards Nemi, the woods reveal themselves for alder only by their catkins.

Immediately above the town of Rocca di Papa, before you begin that ascent through the woods of Monte Cavo, are the Campi d'Annibale, the former crater of the volcano of Mons Latialis, grass fields whose legend Pascarella tells us: that when Hannibal encamped there the Romans raised the necessary money by selling the ground of the enemy's camp! A strange, unexpected place; a great green basin, bleak and bare, marked only by fences like some northern hill-top; on such fell sides shall the Romans camp above the Tyne and Tweed.

We climbed up through the woods, Antonia and I, following the keeper in his riding boots, silent, or at most exchanging a word about the flowers, all blue, borage, squill, and dog violets, among the fallen leaves. And little by little there unrolled, deep below us, the dim green plain with a whiteness which is St. Peter's; and then there unfolded, gradually, unexpected, the pale blue of one lake and of a second. Till, near the top, they had both turned into steely mirrors, tarnished, as by breath, by the rapidly passing clouds. And the pink of the leafless woods stretches away, soft and feathery, to distant towns and villages. And we ascend, with the wind arising to meet us, always through softly winding paths, to the summit of the Latin mountain. To a long, gaunt, white, empty house, a circle of ancient moss-grown walls, a circle of old, wind-bent, leafless beeches, with the whole world of earliest Rome misty below, and thin clouds passing rapidly overhead. This is that sort of natural altar, visible as such even from the streets of Rome, of the Latin Jove, which, when we saw it again later from the ridge near Castel Gandolfo, above the deep circular chasm (fringed with asphodel) of the lake, seemed to smoke with a superhuman sacrifice.

How Renan, in the *Prêtre di Némi*, has rendered, without descriptions, the charm of that outlook towards Rome from this lower portion of the Latin hills! They cover a very small amount of country, volcanic and isolated; they are a kind of living whole in themselves, with their towns, woods, and those two deep lakes hidden in their fastnesses. The most living range of hills, surely, out of which the greatest life has spread, the vastest, perhaps, in the world.

Up there one looks not merely into space unlimited, but into time. What a strange country this Roman one! How different from the rest of Italy; this, with its great plain, its isolated groups of hills, its disdain of river-valley and gorge; a country set aside for different destinies.

And yet I own that what these hills represent most to me is the keenness of the air, the sweetness of those straight-boled, pinkish, leafless woods, the freshness of sprouting grass and flowers.

March 20

IV

A River God

We have been bicycling these two days in the campagna; sunny, windy days, the hills faint in the general blueness. About three miles along the Via Ardeatina we alighted and sat on the grass in a little valley. A little valley between two low grass hills; a stream, a few reeds, two or three scant trees in bud, and the usual fences, leading up to the mountain, framed in, with its white towns, between the green slopes. Grass still short and dry; larks, invisible, singing; a flock of sheep going along with shepherds stopping to set the new-born, tottering lambs to suck.

At the valley's mouth, over a wide horse-trough where a donkey cart was watering, a little recumbent river god, rudely carved and much time-stained.

March 16

V

The Pantheon

A bright day of iciest tramontana, cutting you in two in the square, under the colonnades, and in the narrow chink-opening of the great green bronze doors.

Almost entirely empty, that great round place, the light, the cold haunting its grey dome. At the high-altar some priests in purple; the Crucifix and pictures veiled in violet silk. And in the organ loft, buttoned up in great coats, five wretched musicians; not on high, but in a sort of cage set down by the altar. Such singing! but an alto, two tenors and a bass, as in Marcello's psalms. And, frightful as was the performance, I was fascinated by their unaccompanied song: something of long vague passages, and suspended cadences, fitting, in its mixture of complexity and primitiveness, its very rudeness, barbarousness of execution, into the great round bleak temple, with the cold windy sky looking down its roof, the bleakness of outdoors, enclosed, as it were, within doors.

Palm Sunday, 1899

VI

Santi Quattro Coronati

I went into several small churches to see the sepulchres. Not like our Tuscan ones; wretched things, mainly tinsel and shabby frippery.

At Santa Prisca we trespassed into orchards, almond trees barely green, artichokes and dust-heaps, with the belfries of the Aventine behind, the pillared loggia of San Saba, and the great blocks of the Baths of Caracalla in front. The church, shut on ordinary days, was quite empty, only a dozen Franciscans at office, kneeling by the frame of lighted candles, one of which was extinguished with each verse of hoarse liturgy by a monk kneeling apart.

After Sta. Prisca, San Clemente, very Byzantine and fine in the gloom, and then to that dear church of the Santi Quattro Coronati, which has beckoned to me ever since my childhood; and which, with its fortified-looking apse, its yard and great gate-tower, looks like a remote abbey one would drive to, forgotten, hidden, unheard of, for hours and hours from some out-of-the-way country town. "We'll take you to so and so," one's host would say, and one would never have heard the name before. . . And there it is, above the modernest slums of modern Rome!

The church was darkish; a little light from the sunset just picking out some green and purple of the broken pavement; the tapers of a curtained-off chapel, and tapers above the sepulchre, throwing a broad weak yellow light up to the arched triforium, to the grated gallery whence came the voices of nuns chanting the Lamentations.

From round the illuminated sepulchre rose, like a flock of birds on our entrance, a bevy of kneeling nuns in *béguine* cloak and cap. And in the apse, before the high-altar, was stretched on the slabs, with a night-light at each corner, something dark and mysterious: the crucifix, the form barely defined, shrouded in violet.

When the nuns went away a number of children, tiny, tiny girls came in, and knelt round that veiled mysterious thing; a baby at the end of their procession. One of the little girls could not resist, and lifted a corner of the violet silk. But her elder sister quickly slapped her, pulled her kerchief straight, and all was order and piety.

The dear church, quite empty save for these children, was full of the smell of the fresh flowers round the sepulchre. A holy, fragrant, venerable, kindly church, safe-hidden behind its pillared atrium and gate-tower; and looking from afar like a hillside fortress among the jerry-built modern streets.

Maundy Thursday, 1899

VII

Beyond Pont Molle

A meadow near the Tiber, of grass and daisies, tufted with yellow-hearted jonquils. Larks and sun and wind overhead; in the distance the pale mountains, patched with snow. All round, the pale green embosomings of the soft earth hills. If the Umbrians got their love of circular hill lines at home, they learned in Rome the real existence of the green grass valleys and hills unbroken by cultivation, like those behind Perugino's *Crucifixion* and Spagna's *Muses*.

All round, as I sit in that place, the dry last year's stalks dance in the wind above the new grass and flowers. O Easter, Resurrection, Renovation!

The larks proclaim it!

Easter, 1899

SPRING 1900

I

Outside the Gates

Rome took hold of me again as usual, yesterday, bicycling near Porta S. Sebastiano. On the walls which enclose those remote forsaken vignas (fit abode for lamias and female vampyres, as in Frau von Degen's tale), nay, even on the gates of old Rome are painted great advertisements exhorting the traveller to go to such or such a curiosity shop. The Arch of Drusus was surrounded by a band of Cookites, listening inattentively to their Bear Leader; and the whole Via Appia, to beyond Cecilia Metella, was alive with cabs and landaus. But such things, which desecrate Venice and spoil Florence, are all right in Rome; Rome, somehow, knows how to subdue them all to her eternal harmony. That all the vulgarities of all the furthest lands should all pass through Rome, like all the barbarians, the nations and centuries, seems proper and fit. The spirit of the place requires them, as much as the captives who came in the triumphs, as the Goths and Huns, as the pilgrims of the Mediæval Jubilees, and it subdues them: subdues them, as it subdues with the chemistry of this odd climate of crumble and decay, the new dreadful houses; as it has made, with the marvellous rank Roman vegetation, a sort of Forum or Palatine of the knocked-down modern houses, the empty unfinished basements behind the hoardings under my window. Driving at midnight from the station, my eye and mind were caught not merely by Castor and Pollux under the electric light, and by the endless walls of high palaces, but also by a colossal advertisement of Anzio, in English, setting forth to the traveller its merits connected with Nero, and I think Coriolanus—Nero and Coriolanus as elements of *réclame*!

But here it seems all right; becoming only one of those immense ironies of Time, more dignified than any of Time's paltry creatures of which this place is full. Time, whose presence, whose very cruelties and gigantic jests, brings such peace to the soul in this place. Peace because hope. This litter, this dust-heap (for it is after all not much better, few great or precious or perfect things remaining), dust-heap or rag-fair symbolised by its own most barbarous and vilest and most venerable parts along the Tiber and under the Capitoline,—this Rome accustoms one to take patience and heart of grace. It helps one to conceive the fact that life comes everywhere out of death and subdues it; to feel that, as there are centuries in the Past, so there will be centuries and centuries in the Future. It helps the imagination with its remnants of old, used-up theatre scenes, to guess at all the scene-shifting that will be accomplished, and to take its stand, be it only in the emotion of an instant, as witness of the vague phantasmagoria of the future. Why despair? Why be impatient? only give time, only secure all the possible tickets in the lottery of chance, and our hopes must at last be realised, all will be all right. 'Tis only our miserable impatience, our miserable sense of our own impotent mortality, which makes us fret: and Rome bids us take patience and comfort.

We despair of the future, for one reason, because we attribute to the future our own growing sense of fatigue, the feelings of evening. But the future will, for those to whom it belongs, be morning, with the vigour and buoyancy of the awakening. Our ideal would be to preserve in the future the beautiful things—certain flowers of tradition and privilege—of the past. 'Tis a delusion. We might as well hope to keep the old leaves on the trees into next summer. But after the old leaves have fallen and the trees have stood bare, new ones will come, not the same, but similar.

March 11

II

LATTER-DAY ROME

As a matter of fact Rome has never been so much Rome, never expressed its full meaning so completely, as nowadays. This change and desecration, this inroad of modernness, merely completes its eternity. Goethe has an epigram of a Chinese he met here; but a Chinese of the eighteenth century completed Rome less than an American of the nineteenth. Not only all roads in space, but all roads across Time, converge hither.

March 11

III

Santa Balbina

Went to take the English seeds to the gardener at S. Saba, and got in return some plants of border pinks. The most poetical and real place in all Rome.

Afterwards bicycled to S. Balbina. Impression of primitive church (the outside has from a distance a look as of something in a Pinturicchio fresco) given over to the Franciscan nuns—thirty—who look after two hundred unruly girls off the streets. Their thick grey cloaks are folded on the pews; images, screens, lecterns, all the litter of a priestly lumber-room, poked here and there, a little portable iron pulpit, not unlike a curtained washstand, in front of a beautiful tomb of a grave mediæval person above a delicate mosaic of the Cosmatis, and a small coloured Rue Bonaparte St. Joseph on the episcopal mosaic throne in the apse!

March 15

IV

THE CATACOMBS

Today Catacombs of S. Domitilla in Via Sette Chiese, with Maria, Guido and Pascarella. The impression of walking for miles by taper-light between those close walls of brown friable stone, or that soft dusty ground, in a warm vague stifling air; the monotonous rough sides, the monotonous corners, the widenings in and out of little Galla Placidia-like crypts, with rough hewn pillars and faded frescoes; of the irregularly cut pigeon-holes, where bits of bone moulder, and the brown earth seems half composed of bone.

That brown soft earth of the Catacombs, the stuff you would scratch off the damp walls with your nail; rotting stone, rotting bone: the very soil of Rome lilackish like cocoa, friable, light, which used somehow to give me the horrors already as a child; the soil in which the gardener of S. Saba grows his pinks and freesias without a spade or hoe visible anywhere; the soil which seems to demand no plough; the farthest possible from the honest and stiff clay, demanding human work, of nature; the Roman soil, a *compost*, as Whitman would say, ready manured! The work of man in this earth (of which a pinch transported into church front or roof produces great tufts of fennel and wild mignonette), the work of man in it merely to have died!

No sense of the ages in these Catacombs, or of the solemnity of death, or of the sweetness of religion; black narrow passages gutted for centuries, the poor wretched human remains (save those few turned up by the modern spade) packed, sent off, made presents of, sold to all the churches and convents of Christendom; bits of bones in cotton wool, with faded labels, in glass cases, such as we see in sacristies, &c., or enclosed in glories of enamel and gold!

But all gone, gone, those poor humble inhabitants, who were so anxious to be entire for the resurrection of the body!—patrician ladies, slaves, soldiers, eunuchs, theologians—all gone piecemeal all over the distant earth! the corridors swept and empty, the pigeon-holes with only a little brown cocoa-like dust!

It was raining all day, dull, dismal. Yet coming out of that place, out of that brown crumbly darkness, what was not the interest of the wet grey sky! How great the beauty, the movements of the lazy clouds! How complex and lovely the bare lane of wattled dry reeds—the ineffable exquisiteness of patches of green corn, of a few scant pink blossoms, of the shoots of elder! I remember the solemnity of the subterranean tombs at Perugia; the grisliness of the Beauchamp crypt at Warwick. But these catacombs, emptiness, desolation and that old brown lilacky, crumbly Roman earth, in which no plough need move nor spade,—that *terriccio*, that pot-mould of the past.

March 16

V

The Rione Monti

Yesterday, in gusty weather, wandered round muddy streets of Rione Monti, and entered some churches. S.S. Cosmae Damiano in Forum: it has got lost, so to speak, in the excavations, and you seek it through blind alleys and a long dark passage—a dirty, tawdry church, with a few frowsy, sluttish people; and behind the ballroom chandeliers above the altar, a Ravenna apse, gold and blue; and lambs in procession on a green ground.

Then S. Pietro in Vincoli, which has a delightful position, with its big palm and tower and a certain Romantic Catherine Sforza character; also, what always refreshes me in Rome, its early Renaissance character, before Jesuits, &c. &c., an imported thing from Tuscany, and the fact of the tomb of the Pollajuolos! Michel Angelo's *Moses* somehow belongs to Rome—has Rome's grandeur, emphasis, and Rome's theatrical quality. All round are buried seventeenth-century prelates. Cinthio Aldobrandini, &c., setting forth glories, but with skeletons as supporters!

Decidedly Rome was never more Roman than at present—the pulling down and building and excavating, the inappropriate jostlings of time and character merely add to the eternal quality, serene and ironical. Besides, these demolitions have disclosed many things hitherto hidden, and soon destroyed: here in Rione Monti, for instance, above the tram-lines, great green walls, boulders from Antiquity, and quiet convent gardens, with spaliered lemons, suddenly displayed above the illustrated hoardings of a street to be. In the midst of it, in a filthy, half modern, crowded street, a rugged Lombard church porch, dark ages all over: the object of my search, St. Praxed's church; but it was walled up, and I entered by a door in a side lane. Entered to remain on threshold, a Mass at a side altar. Eight small boys blocking the way, with a crowd of sluttish, tawdry worshippers, with the usual Roman church stifling dirty smell. These Roman churches, all save the basilicas, are inconceivably ill kept, frowsy, musty, tawdry, sluttish: they belong not to God, but to Rome—the same barbarous Rome of the tumble-down houses, the tattered begging people, the whole untidy squalor of its really Roman parts. Nothing swept and garnished; nothing evincing one grain of past or present reverence—a down-at-heel indifferent idolatry. At last the crowd streamed out, Mass being over, and I entered—and, oh wonder! found myself in a place of all Byzantine splendour: that little chapel, tapestried with crimson silk, lit with hanging lamps, its vaults a marvellous glory of golden—infinite tinted golden—mosaics with great white angels. A bit of Venice, of S. Mark's in this sluttish Rome.

Poets really make places. I cannot pass the Consolazione Hospital without thinking of Pompilia's death there; and the imaginary bishop, of whom there is no visible trace, haunts Sta. Prassede.

VI

AMPHORÆ

In the afternoon we went to the Via Appia, and in the excavations of Villa Lugari, among sprouting corn and under the song of larks, saw those amphoræ Pascarella had told us of, which, after holding pagan wine, were used to bury Christian children. To me there is nothing repulsive in the thought of this burial in the earth's best product.

VII

MASS AT THE LATERAN

Today, on the way to Porta Furba (the country, where one sees it near the gate, is beginning to be powdered over with peach blossom), I went into the Lateran, and heard and saw a beautiful canonical Mass. Here was the swept and garnished (but it was behind glass doors!) sanctuary, the canons dainty in minever, a splendid monsignore, grey-haired, in three shades of purple; exquisite white and gold officiating priests, like great white peacocks, at the altar; the perfect movement of the incensing, perfect courtesy and dignity of the mutual salutations; and a well-played organ, on a reed stop, giving an imitation Bach *musette*. The whole ceremony, rather like the 6/8 of that *musette*, perhaps a trifle too much of the dancing element, but grave and very perfect. Why should not, at some future period, our philosophers sit in carved oak stalls, in minever and purple, and salute and be saluted, and speak with intervals of *musettes* on the organ? It would suit Renan at least; and surely this, which is so venerable and sanctioned by time in our eyes, would have seemed quite as odd and grotesque a thing if foretold to St. Paul.

VIII

Stage Illusion

I feel that, among other good things, Rome, while it gave my childhood notions of dignity, of time and solemn things, kept my eye and fancy on very short commons. How stunted are the trees (all except the weeds) here! How flowerless the hedges! How empty of life, grace, detail the country!

I remember the sort of rapture of the first acquaintance with Tuscan valleys, hills, woods, fields, and all the lovely fulness of dainty real detail.

Rome, as I said before, is all theatre scenes; marvellous *coup d'oeils*, into which, advancing (from the Capitol) from opposite the Palatine palms, from the Lateran steps, from the Tiber quays, you find nothing *to go on with*; and in so far it fits, it symbolises, perhaps, its own history—for what is history but a series of such admirable theatrical views; mere delusion, and behind them prose, mere prose? The reality of Rome is, one feels it, in its distant hills. There you can penetrate; thence history streamed.

March 19

IX

SANTA MARIA IN COSMEDIN

After wandering between tremendous hailstorms about the Aventine (the black sky and turbid Tiber from S. Alessio, in odd contrast with the lemons and oranges and freesias of S. Sabina, and with the chill empty churches), I waited for a Mass at S. M. in Cosmedin. Garlands (how poor and inartistic compared to the Tuscan and Venetian ones!) hanging in porch and box strewn at the door. The church, just restored, very swept and garnished still, with its Byzantine delicacy of fluted ribbed columns, carved precious ambones and carpet of lovely marbles, a place for the perfect ritual and splendid vestments of an aristocratic worship, slowly filled with, oh! such a poor, poor, wretched congregation, while the two priests, two sacristans and small choir-boys looked on (with a glance at watch) like people preparing for a play and waiting for a full house; the bell-ringer occasionally hanging on to the rope near the door, and giving a jump as he let go. I don't mean merely poor in fortune, in ragged draggled clothes, the sweepings of those rag-fair quarters, but poor in wretched, ill-grown, ill, dull, stupid bodies and souls, draggle-tailed like their clothes, only two savage-looking peasants having dignity or grace. More like an Irish congregation than an Italian, the two policemen, the women nursing their babies, the dreary sickly nuns, the broken, idiot-looking shabby elderly men in overcoats.

At last the priests and choir-boys, to match, went in procession to the altar, and the service began; merely chants with a response from the crowd. But as soon as they began everything seemed to pull together, to be all right, to have significance. . .

Is it possible that of religious things only the æsthetic side is vital, universal, is what gives or seems to give a meaning, deludes us into a belief in some spirituality? Sometimes one suspects as much: that the unifying element is not so much religion, as, after all, art.

March 23

X

INSCRIPTIONS

These are fragments of inscriptions from the Macellus Liviæ, of the time of Valens and Gratian, now transferred to the porch of S. Maria in Trastevere: "Maceus vixit dulcissime cum suis ad supremam diem. C. Gannius primogenitus vix: ann. VII. Desine jam mater lacrimis rinovare querellas—namque dolor talis non tibi contigit uni." So at least I read.

Another states that "M. Cocceius Ambrosius Aug: Lib: præpositus vestis albæ triumphalis (?) fecit." When he had lived with Nice (?) his wife forty-five years eleven days "sine ulla querela."

Also, "Dis Manib. Rhodope fecerent (?) Berenice et Drusilla delicatæ dulcissimæ suae (*sic*)."

Also, "Attidiæ felicissimæ uxori rariosimæ Fl: Antoninus."

How these inscriptions, of which I copied out a few yesterday during a heavy shower in the portico of S. M. in Trastevere, make one feel, again by this magic of Rome, the other half of the truth: How little the centuries matter, how vain are these thousands of years, which exist only in our thoughts, how solely important are the brief pangs of us poor obscure shortlived forgotten creatures!

March 30

Palazzo Orsini, Formerly Savelli

This is the most Roman house, in my sense, of all Rome. The first evening, when I came into my room, the sunset streaming in, the lights beginning below, it was fantastic and overwhelming. What I said of this being a unique moment in Roman history—the genius of the city stripped of all veils, visible everywhere, is especially true about the view from this window. During my childhood Rome was closed, uniform, without either the detail or the panoramic efforts which speak to the imagination; and ten or fifteen years hence the great gaps will be filled up, and the deep historical viscera, so to speak, of the city closed and grown together. Now, with the torn-down houses, the swept-away quarters, one has not only views of hills and river and bridges, and of gardens and palaces and loggias, hidden once and to be hidden again, but into the very life of the people: the squalor of back streets revealed, of yards looked into, of the open places turned into *immondezzaio* and play and grazing ground, showing the barbarism and nakedness of the land—showing one that there is here no tradition of anything more active, decent or human than this present demolition. And the *Sventramento* also reveals the past! From my window, under that sunset behind the trees and fountains and churches of the Janiculum, I look down on a sort of mediæval city of the Trastevere—upon a still stranger, imaginary one made by perspective and fancy; the old bridge, with its two double *hermes* leading between towers, and the long prison-like walls of the inland buildings, into an imaginary square—an imaginary city with more towers, more Romanesque belfries. This is a case of the imaginary place due to perspective, to bird's-eye view, to some reminiscence. (I trace a resemblance to the arsenal gate at Venice, perhaps also to the inner town at Castelfranco.) This case is an illustration of how large a part illusion, even recognised as such, plays in our feeling.

And similarly as regards the *invisible* view. Here am I, in a house nesting in the theatre of Marcellus, the little orange and lemon garden presumably built actually onto those remaining black arches in which coppersmiths and coopers and saddlers, all the humble trades of a backward little country town or village, have burrowed: the thought of Virgil's line with it all. The mangy green grass in front, where the children fly kites and the inconceivable skeleton horses graze, is the site of the former Ghetto; and behind its remaining synagogue, the little belfry, the houses of the Cencis, are down at heel carts and ragged peasants round the little isolated Ghetto fountain; and on the other side the Aventine, the bridge of—was it Cocles? a land of ballad, of popular romance, of tragedy.

March 30

SPRING 1901

I

Quomodo Sedet. . .

Appalling morning of wind and dust; I bicycled in agitation of spirit to Domine quo Vadis. A wretched little church, no kind of beauty about it, full of decayed, greasy pictures, and, far better than they, penny coloured prints of the Saviour and Infant Baptist, and of the Life and Death of the Religious and the Irreligious Person about 1850, both in high hats and tail-coats. The old custodian crone tells me she is half blind, and envies me my glasses. She points out a bit of fresco: "Questo è Gesu Nazzareno"—as the housekeeper might say, "This is the present Earl"—also points out the marble copy of the slab bearing the print of *i suoi santissimi piedi*, square little feet, of such a squat, fat, short-jointed Christ, about as miraculous or venerable as the pattern on a pat of butter.

Turning my face, in that tornado of dust, towards Rome, its walls stretch suddenly before me across the vineyards and fields, broken walls, of any mediæval city you please, and hiding, it would seem, emptiness behind them. The desolation of this distant city, with its foreground of squalid hovels, and ill-favoured wine shop and smithies where the very inscriptions, "Vino di Marino," or "Ferracocchio," or "Ova di Giornata," look as if a megalomaniac, escaped from an asylum, had dipped a brush into a paint-pot and splashed all over; this foreground of vague tombs, masonry heaven knows what, all flowered with huge wild mignonette; this other moving background of ragged peasants and unutterable galled horses; the desolation of this dead city which I feel behind those mediæval walls comes home to them, like the sting of the dust whirlpools and roar of the wind. *Quomodo sedet sola civitas*!

Meanwhile, close to one of those city gates, is a poster announcing lectures "Sur le costume des Premiers Chrétiens!"

But not less incongruous, behind those walls of Rome, are all of us, bringing our absurd modernnesses, our far-fetched things of civilisation into the solemn, starved, lousy, silent Past! At moments like these I feel that one needs be entirely engrossed either in making two ends meet (a clerk or shopkeeper, or one of these haranguing archæologists holding forth under the Arch of Drusus) for his dinner or in tea parties and "jours," and "sport," to endure the company of Rome.

I went into the vigna of S. Cesario for the key of the church. It is the place where there is a small fifteenth-century villa, with those mullioned windows like Palazzo di Venezia, and a little portico, seeming to tell, among the rubbish heaps and onions, of Riario and Borgia suppers. And in this church and the neighbouring one the impression of the inscriptions recording succession of popes and cardinals, all the magnificent locusts who came swarm after swarm, to devour this land, leaving the broken remains of their hurried magnificence, volutes, plaster churches, and, inscriptions! inscriptions!

April 13

II

Villa Falconieri

Villa Falconieri, Frascati—abandoned, overgrown—the wonderful outline of huge Mondragone, with its pines against the mountains. All these villas near each other, and while they open up into the hill and woods (the lovely delicate rose of the budding chestnuts) are still almost within hail of the little town across the valley. So different from the Tuscan villa, even the grandest, say Mte. Gufoni, which is only the extended *fattoria*, its place chosen by the accident of agricultural business. This mouldering rococo villa is inhabited in summer by the Trappists of Tre Fontane, of that Abbey of St. Anastasia which was the suzerain of all Maremma, great part of Umbria and the Tuscan islands! At the end of their miserably cultivated little *orto*, presiding over the few leeks and garlics, on the balustrade towards Rome of all divinities, who but Hortorum Deus!

Near Grottaferrata in a flat green field, a nun, all in white, was seated under one of the big olives: a curious biblical figure.

April 26

III

Porta Latina

Yesterday with P. D. P. at Porta Latina. He told me an extraordinary thing. In the blocked-up arch of that suppressed gate, at the end of a blind alley, an old old couple—a man of ninety and a woman of eighty, had taken up their abode for months; helped occasionally by the monks of the neighbouring convent (with pretty rose-garden) of S. Giovanni a Porta Latina, to whom however permission was refused (the Superior referring to the Card. Vicar and the Card. Vicar to *his* Confessor) to give a roof to the couple because of the woman; also there was a suspicion that the couple had not been married in church. All this P. D. had learned when these people were still there, in the arch. But we found them gone; and the strangest sight instead. In the immense thickness of the gate a heap of reeds in a corner; and strewn all about in this artificial grotto, old rusty utensils, a grater, a strainer, broken pots, papers, rags, half-burnt logs, a straw hat, and a walking stick! And over a kind of recess, on a plank, a little shrine, two broken Madonnas picked out of some dust-heap, withered flowers in a crock, and a sprig of olive, evidently of last Palm Sunday! Poor little properties, so poor, so wretched that they had remained unmolested, despised even by the poorest, safe at the end of that blind road in that closed-up gate of Rome! That two human beings in our day should have lived there for months, even years (for they returned after an absence, the monk told us); lived, like some anchorites of old, in the ruins, in a grotto made by human hands; with the vineyards all round, and the shrubs and flowers waving from the broken masonry! Their rags and shreds of paper littered the rank grass and acanthus by the walled-up gate, where the little Bramantesque temple stands, built by a French prelate under Julius II, and inscribed "Au plaisir de Dieu." *Au plaisir de Dieu!*

Over the walls, the great bones of the Baths of Caracalla half hidden by trees: and, closing the distance, St. Peters. We went into the little damp church, with a twelfth-century campanile and well in the rose-garden; a deserted little place, only a bit of opus Alexandrinum, and a string of Cosmati work remaining, all the rest overlaid by the frescoes and stuccoes of a seventeenth-century Rasponi. The grey Franciscan who showed us round told us that a lady had given five hundred francs for admission of the old man and woman of the gate at the Petites Soeurs; but these required the religious marriage. About a month ago the couple was married and taken off to the Petites Soeurs; the day after the poor old man died! The old people had desired the monks to distribute their bedding and rags to the poor, now they themselves were provided for. And that is how the place came to be abandoned. The old man told the monks he much preferred the arch to the damp cellar where a greengrocer of Rome used to make him sleep. "They had good sides those people," I remarked. "Sfido! bonissimi," said the Franciscan; he was from Albi, but had got to speak with a Roman accent.

While we were there, under the impression of that story, of the deserted church, the ragged grey monk, and of that whole squalid, imaginative Roman corner, a little cart drove up with a young man and two little girls, who went round with us and gathered sprays of hawthorn off the walls, leaving the pony to graze meanwhile. "No Romans," said P. D.; and indeed they turned out to be Vicentines, the young man a student of law taking out his young cousins for a *scampagnata*. P. D. very characteristically made them write their names for him in his pocket-book, and bowed to the little girls as if they were duchesses. More characteristically still, my friend carried off the old beggar's stick to keep in his study.

April 26

SPRING 1902

I

The Rubbish-Heap

Yesterday wandered in Trastevere and about Piazza Mattei and Montanara and back by bus; again this morning tramm'd to Lateran in showers. The squalor of this Rome and of its people! The absence of all trace of any decent past, ancient barbarism as down at heel and unkempt as any modern slum! The starved galled horses, broken harness, unmended clothes and wide-mouthed sluttishness under the mound on which stand the Cenci's houses, a foul mound of demolition and rag-pickers, only a stone's-throw from the brand-new shop streets, the Lungo Tevere, the magnificence of palaces like the Mattei, Caetani, &c. If Rome undoubtedly gives the soul peace by its assurance that the present is as nothing in the centuries, it also depresses one, in other moods, with the feeling that all history is but a vast rubbish-heap and sink; that nothing matters, nothing comes out of all the ages save rags and brutishness. There is a great value for our souls in any place which tells us, by however slight indications, of a past of self-respect, activity and beauty; and I long for Tuscany.

February 25

II

THE EXCAVATIONS

In the Forum this morning with Css. B. and the excavator Boni. In the Director's shed a "Campionario," literally pattern sheets of the various strata of excavation: bits of crock, stone, tile, iron, little earthenware spoons for putting sacrificial salt in the fire, even what looked like a set of false teeth. Time represented thus in space. And similarly with the excavations themselves: century under century, each also represented by little more than foot-prints, bases of gone columns, foundations of rough edifices. Among these neatly-dug-out layers of nothingness, these tidy heaps of chips with so few things, stand out the few old column- and temple-ends which Piranesi already drew.

I felt very keenly that the past is only a creation of the present. Boni, a very interesting and ardent mind, poetical and mystical, showed us things not really of this earth, not really laid bare by the spade, but existing in realms of fantastic speculation, shaped by argument, faultlessly cast in logical moulds. Too faultlessly methought, for looking at the mere heaps of architectural rubbish, let alone the earth, the various vegetations which have accumulated upon it, I had a sense of the infinite intricacy of all reality, and of the partiality and insufficiency of the paths which our reason (or our fancy in the garb of reason) cuts into it. Rituals and laws whose meaning had become mere shibboleths two thousand years ago, races whose very mien and aspect (often their language) can only be speculated on: all this reappears, takes precision and certainty. But is not this a mere creation, like that of art or of systematic metaphysics? What struck me as the only certainty among these admirable cogent arguments was that the once tank of Juturna, round whose double springs Rome must have arisen to drink and worship, this sacred and healing water where the Dioscuri watered their steeds after Lake Regillus, has been fouled by human privies so deeply that years of dredging and pumping will be required to restore its purity. Of how many things is not this tank a symbol as cogent as any which our archæologist ascribed to those old symbol-mongers of his discourse!

With us was a man who took no interest in all these matters; none in the significance of rituals, symbols, or the laws of racial growth and decadence. *He* wanted to be shown the place where Cæsar had fallen; he was a survivor of the old school of historical interest. Very out of date and droll; but is not this old-fashioned interest in half-imaginary dramatic figures as legitimate as our playing with races, rituals, the laws, the metaphysical essence of the past?

February 27

III

The Meet

The meet the other day, at Maglianella, beyond Porta S. Pancrazio. Desolate, rolling country, pale green wide dells, where streams should be, but are not; roads excavated in the brown volcanic rock, here and there fringed with a few cork-trees; the approach, very much, to Toscanella. But raced along by carriages, bicycles and motor-cars, and leading to a luncheon tent, a car full of hounds, school of cavalry officers, and the redcoats preparing to start. The cloud banks sat on the horizon as on the sea; the sky very pale and blue, moist, with song of larks descending from it. And as the horses cantered along the soft grass, the scent of last year's mint and fennel rose from stubble-fields, and the rank, fresh smell of crushed succulent asphodels.

February 27

IV

The cabman who, yesterday evening, took me to Palazzo Gabbrielli instead of Palazzo Orsini, excused himself saying that priests even blunder at the altar—"anche li preti sbajano all altare." Very Roman!

V

Monte Mario

With E. de V. on Monte Mario. The weather has cleared; slight tramontana, pure sky, with white storm- or snow-clouds collected like rolled-up curtains, everywhere on the horizon. Great green slopes of grass appear as far as one could see, here and there a little valley full of ilex scrub; in the mist of the distance conical shepherds' huts, with smoke wreath. We sat on a piece of turf, cut in by horses' hoofs, by a stack of faggots; song of lark and bleating of sheep. But for the road, the carriage, it might have been in the Maremma for utter loneliness and freshness. Turning round a few yards further, carriages and motor-cars, and all Rome, with its unfinished new quarters nearest, stretched under us.

March 3

VI

Via Ostiense

Day before yesterday with dear Paso along Via Ostiense. Perhaps the most solemn of all those solemn Roman roads, with the solemnity and desolation of the great brimful brown Tiber, between barren banks of mud, added to the solemnity of the empty green country. It is the refusal of vegetation in great part which makes this country strange and solemn. Such vegetation as there is, the asphodels and rare blackthorn along the road, the stumpy oaks or cork-trees or the bends of the river, gaining an importance, a significance out of all proportion; and the thinnest little distant spinny, looking like a mysterious consecrated wood. We got to the top of a hill, and there, far off against the grey flatness, was the lavender line of the sea. It was a brilliant day of freshly fallen distant snow; the air keen and windless, with a feel of the sea as we went towards it.

VII

Palace Yards

Yesterday P. D. P. took me to see a former Marescotti palace in the Via della Pigna. A very quiet aristocratic part of Rome, of narrow streets between high palaces, and little untraversed squares. The gloominess of the outside succeeded by the sunlight, the spaciousness of a vast courtyard, on to which look sixteenth-, seventeenth-, eighteenth-century windows, closed by the back of a church with its clock-tower, so that, as Pierino says, it might almost be the piazza of a provincial town. A campanile, fountain, piazza, almost a *sun*, all to oneself. One wonders with what these palaces could ever have been filled by the original owners.

We then went into another palace yard; and there was a shop with three young men working at a huge sawdust doll, with porcelain sandalled feet. I thought it was a doll for displaying surgical apparatus, but it turned out to be a female saint, whose head we were shown, life-size, properly expressive with rolling eyes and a little halo.

March 6

SPRING 1903

I

Return to Rome

That I should feel it most on return here; find I have returned without *her*, travelled without her, that she is not there to tell; the sense of utter loneliness, of the letter one would write, the greeting one would give—and which no creature now wants!

Yesterday morning, feeling ill and very sad, Rome came for half-hour with its odd consolation. I sat on the balcony of the corner room, very high up, in the sunshine. Cabs, with their absurd Roman canter, crossing the diaper of the little square, circling, as I remember them doing in my childhood, round the unwilling fare. A soldier rode across, dismounted, took his beast by the bridle to the cattle-trough in the palace wall opposite; a bit of campagna intruded into town. And motor-cars snorted and bells rang. High up on the same level with me was the hidden real Rome—all that you do not guess while walking in the streets below. Colonna gardens with bridges over the way, and green-clipped hedges and reddening Judas-trees under the big pines, and a row of marble Emperors turning their backs; and, further, the Quirinal with tip of obelisk, and plaster trumpet-blowing Fame; and a palm-tree, its head rising out of I know not what hidden yard, in front of a terrace of drying rags. And at every vista end, pines of the Pincian, Villa Doria, &c.; and domes; and the pale blond roofs with the telephone wires like gossamer stretched over them. Sunshine; distant noise and incessant bells. Rome in a fashion consoling; but how empty!

April 3

II

Palm Sunday

This morning I know not what ceremony in the Portico of SS. Apostoli: a little procession, some monks, a priest in purple, and a few draggle-tailed people before the closed door, chanting at intervals, till the door opened and they entered, their silver cross in its purple bag ahead, and their little branches of olive. The fine carved Roman eagle in its magnificent garland of oak-leaves, presiding, very fierce and contemptuous, over this little scene. When one effaces the notion of habit, how very odd to see a company of nineteenth-century people, battered and galled by life like old cab-horses, stationing in a portico singing verses and holding branches of olive! There is something refreshing, something of the fields and hills, of leisure and childishness, in the proceeding, if only the poor creatures realised it. But to most of them, I take it, the bearing of a silver cross, of an olive branch, is in reality as utilitarian (though utilitarian in regard to another world) as holding the tail of a saucepan or rattling a money-box. For how many, one wonders, is that door, opening to the cross and the olive branches, the door of an inner temple, of a place swept and garnished in the pious fancy? alas! alas!

I went on, on foot, past the Capitol, through the Montanara region, with a growing sense, which I have had ever since return here, of the squalor, the lousiness, the dust-heap, the unblushing *immondezzaio* quality of Rome and its inhabitants. Everything ragged, filthy, listless; the very cauliflowers they were selling looking all stalk, fit for that refuse midden which symbolises the city. By the Temple of Vesta a lot of carts were drawn up, with galled horses and ragged crouching peasants—that sort of impression which Piranesi gives.

A school of little girls, conducted by a nun, was filing out of S. Maria in Cosmedin, and I helped up the leathern curtain for them to pass. Tatters, squalor, with that abundant animal strength and beauty of these people; one feels they have been eating and drinking, and befouling the earth and the streets with the excrements of themselves and their lives, love-making and begetting, and suffering stolidly all through the centuries, and one wonders why? as one wonders before a ditch full of tadpoles. Low mass was going on at a side altar, and the canon's mass in the beautiful marble choir, behind the ambones, behind those delicate marble railings and seats, which, with their inclusion, makes the fine aristocratic, swept and garnished quality of that Byzantine architecture more delicate and dainty still. The church was finished restoring two years ago, but the population of that low part of Rome, the Piazza Montanara St. Giles, has already given it the squalor of ages. I cannot say how deeply, though vaguely, I felt the meaningless tragic triviality of these successive generations of reality, in the face of that solemn, meaningful abstraction which we call history, which we call humanity, the centuries, Rome.

The great holes through which, as through earthquake rents, the innermost life of Rome has become visible in the last thirty years, are beginning to close up. In that sort of rag-fair, witch-burning ground limited only by the island and the belfries of Trastevere which I used to look down upon from Palazzo Orsini, the Jews are building a colossal synagogue. One does not grudge it them, after their Holy Cross Days! But that strange simultaneous vision of the centuries (like that of their life which drowning folk are said to have) is ending with the death agony of old Rome.

April 4

III

MONDRAGONE

The white peacocks apparently all gone; but two superb green ones, their tails outspread, glittering on the grass under the olives just below the villa terrace. Near the terrace, where a lot of olive wood was being chopped on a stump of fine fluted column, a bay-tree of the girth of a good-sized oak, bearing pale yellow leaves and blossom, as of beaten metal, the golden bough of the Sibyl. Hard by another bay-tree, a ramping python, rearing up a head of bright green leaves. The loveliness of the chestnut woods on the hill behind, not yet in leaf, but rosy with rising sap; big round olives also, dark silver in front. The same colours and same wonderful rounded dimpled volcanic lie of the land as round Villa Lante at Viterbo. We walked, the Carlo R's little governess and I, along round above Mondragone and down by Villa Falconieri; the three children on donkeys in front, Gabriella's boys and their cousins. The pleasantness of the children's voices, of their bear-fighting in the train coming back. A splendid day of sun, wind, of dove's-wing distant Campagna view.

April 14

IV

SAN SABA

S an Saba today, for the second time this year, with those pleasant English people the P.s. It was Thursday, and we were not admitted into the garden (though we were very kindly allowed into the loggia) because the pupils of the Germanic College were having their weekly recreation, a hundred of them. We saw their gowns, like geraniums or capsicums, moving between the columns and under the blossoming orange-trees. And a party of them sat among the fallen pillars and broken friezes outside the little churches singing—and what?—the Lorelei in chorus, "Sie kämmt sich mit goldenem Kamme und singt ein Lied dabei." Oh, friendly romance of Germany, lurking even in the house of the Lord, and cheek-by-jowl with De Propaganda Fide!

PAL. SCIARRA, *April* 16

V

A Convent

This morning with Antonia at S. Cecilia in Trastevere, having a special permission from Minister to see the Cavalieri frescoes in the nuns' choir gallery (like poorer, clumsier, *jowlier* Duccio; Byzantine, with antique braided hair and "Greek" features). The impression of the convent *clausura*—little vestibule, a strongly grated small window inside it, apparently ending only in darkness; the "Ruota," behind which a voice spoke mysteriously as through a telephone, the wooden shelf turning on itself and offering us a key—key opening (by instructions of mysterious voice) an adjacent small room: two straw chairs on either side of small table before a thick black grating; another grating behind that, and a kind of perforated shutter between. The latter rattled away, a nun's face uncertainly seen—faded cheeks, immense eyes, white dress, behind the black double bars; the key restored to the Ruota, and engulfed after directions from the mysterious voice; another door, sound of keys and bolts. In all this a predominant and lugubrious impression of keys and bolts. The little portress, Donna Maria Geltude (for these nuns are Benedictines, and have the handle to their names), a wizen, very ugly little woman, in incredibly shabby but spotless dress, white wool washed threadbare to an appearance of linen, voluminous skirts and black veil. A glazed cloister (with twelfth-century columns), a few pictures, seventeenth-century tables and chairs, as in a passage; more passages similar, with *prie Dieu* and scant peasant furniture. The little library, a smallish glass press with nothing but Filotea, Fr. de Sales, Vite dei Santi, &c. Might they read them? Yes, but only on asking the Abbess. Terror of nun lest Antonia and I should go on or into anything not mentioned in our permit—the impression that in this life all can be done, but done only by permission. "Men allowed to visit?" Only by permission of Cardinal Segretario di Stato. "Men working in garden, masons, &c.?" Yes, but always with special permission; permission and bars!

In all these corridors and stairs not a creature; only at one moment a door stirred, Antonia thought she saw a nun?? Little garden, with box hedges and lemon-trees. The inner windows (cells) open on this garden, are large, ordinary, and without bars. There was even one long ground floor window with a little balcony and steps with a cat on them. But never a soul! Great bareness, fair neatness, and order.

The gilt box of the choir, looking down into church; the stalls; the Abbess's gold-headed crozier stuck into her stall (St. Cecilia with harp in it), two lecterns with Latin lessons of the day—the day's martyrology.

April 22

VI

Colonna Gardens

With Contessa Z. today in Colonna Gardens. Great surprise on finding them more romantic than from the outside. A terrace, with all Rome, blond; all manner of unexpected towers and cupolas. The pines of the Janiculum, staircase fountains, waterless but noisy, the Roman veil of vegetation everywhere; and great vague walls of spaliered roses and lemons. In the midst of these terraces and balustrades and crowded nurseries of flowers, the surprise of finding that that great vague building I have noticed from below is a ruin, roofless, full of wild fig, a castle's square keep. Mediæval? antique? the place surely whence the imaginary Nero watched the burning, and harped!

April 25

VII

PALO

Palo Beach yesterday; motored there by my French friends. I have had fever some days past, and there was more than mere pleasure and amusement in sitting on the sand and breathing the clean cloudless sea-air, instead of the scirocco stuff we had left, alternately simmering and shivering in Rome. By the way, how little the sea gives to Rome (except at the Aventine corner sometimes by a violent libeccio), and how one feels the futility of this tideless Mediterranean, unable to purify or renovate even a few yards of the inland! Think of the estuaries of the North! of the cleansing vivifying tides and draughts which the ocean thrusts into the very vitals of the countries!

No one, one feels, ever landed (since Æneas and his companions) upon this shallow strand, save the raiding Saracens and Barbary pirates, against whom the castle, the martello tower, barely more of Palo, was built. For there is not even here what represents the life of the Mediterranean, the jutting rocks, the sucking in of sea, by the cliffs, the sudden squalls of the stony coasts where sea and land really play and fight together, waves leaping tower-high, and battering at hillsides and swirling in and out of creeks. Here, one understands that a storm would mean mere passive submerging: the water rising higher, covering the straight narrow beach, the low green fields, noiselessly, and retreating when so inclined, with neat stacks of seaweed and samphire left behind. The renovation of Rome, like its drinking water, has always come from the mountains; the Tiber mouth is their outlet, not the inlet of the sea. And the mountain clouds change in shape, stagnate and brood in this low trough; the mountain air faints, dies, in these fever levels.

The beach of Palo is only a few yards wide: a low natural wall of corroded tufo, covered with no maritime bent, but ordinary grass; a line of sea refuse, a band of fine black sparkling sand, and little waves fringed black with that mournful sand, breaking feebly against it. A high sky, with a few sailing clouds; and in it, rather than on the sea, some boats, like toy ducks, on the offing, motionless. We sat on the sand, digging into its moist warmth, and amused (I at least) that this glittering beach left no trace on the land; making Carpaccio St. George

Dragons (with inserted eyes of sand flint) out of blistered drift-wood; and looking about, later, for bits of antique marble and brick upon the sands. For this lazy sea appears to wash no pebbles of its own bringing, but only fragments of stone brought by man, broken off man's buildings, shot by him into the Tiber, in the days, no doubt, when columns were sawed into discs and smashed into petal-shaped wedges for the *Opus Alexandrinum*. I don't think we saw one natural looking stone upon that beach; everything seemed vaguely, precious and outlandish, basalt, porphyry, agate, Rossoantique, and serpentine still bearing its original polish; also fine white marble, Mme. B. possessing a beautiful piece of salty Parian found there, and shaped delicately, curved and bossy, into a perfect heart, the heart of a marble Artemis or Amazon. This the lazy Roman sea does, and it is surely an unusual feat: roll its shingle into vague shapes of symbolic hearts, hearts of serpentine, of jasper, of various beautiful rose and lilac breccias, of basalt, and of fine rose brick, all scattered on the glittering black sand (with funny mourning edges of violet shells), and in the lip of those little black waves. But far more beautiful and extraordinary and brilliant (and to me far more wonderful and odd) was the still uncorrupted little corpse of a kingfisher: sky-blue breast, greenish turquoise ruff, and glossy dark back, lying in state, as dead birds do.

April 29

VIII

Fiumicino

Three days ago, in heavy rain, taken in motor to Fiumicino. Impression of grass, yellow with buttercups, soused with rain, opening, falling aside as we swish noiselessly into it, under the moving dark sky. Magliana: a big farm; one takes a minute in the soaking filthy yard, among manure and litter, to recognise that this dilapidated, leprous-looking building is a palace, with mullioned fifteenth-century windows and coats of arms and inscriptions of Cibo and Riario popes. From the top of the wide low-stepped staircase (like that, also of the Cibo's originally, of Pal. Ruffo), wide views of meadows of pale rumpled grass, yellow here, and there with clover, and a great yellow Tiber arm unaccountable in this sort of England. This is the place, I believe, where the quails are shot and netted at this time of year; and I suppose Leo X was on some such expedition when he caught his death here.

Fiumicino, a canal or arm of the Tiber, a yellowish marsh, a big, uprooted looking martello tower by the beach, and a little pier with a green boat like a beetle in the rain. The look of Viareggio or Porto Corsini, of all the little God-forsaken and strangled harbours of this country. The sacred island, I suppose, on the other side of a bridge of boats, covered with what seems a scrub of ilex and lentisk.

IX

Via Ardeatina

Yesterday, again in pelting rain, far along Via Ardeatina (the brutes have taken away the little river god from off that trough in the little valley of poplars). The hollows full of foaming yellow streams, and yellow water gushing everywhere. The great wet green slopes under the dark low sky, with only sheep and here and there a stump of masonry, no trees, no hedges, no walls save of rough stones, no bounding mountains, visible; the whole country transformed into some northern high-lying moorland. A sort of tiny half-ruined, towered and walled St. Gimignano, with many olives about it, seems a ghostly apparition in it all.

May 3

X

SAN TEODORO

This morning, trying to lose time before lunching at Monte Savella, I was attracted into that little round brick church nearly always closed, which stands in a circular hole under the Palatine. You go down a flight of steps into a round paved place: and this, with a worn-down sacrificial altar, carved with laurel wreaths, was strewn this morning with ivy leaves and bay. Lifting the big green drapery which had first attracted me to that church, for it hung outside it, and pushing the door, there was a shock of surprise; a plunge into mystery. The round church was empty, dark, but full of the smell of fresh incense; and in that darkness I was fairly blinded by the effulgence of the high-altar, tier upon tier of tapers. When I was able to see, there were three women, black, with red scapulars about their necks, kneeling; and on either side, in the extreme corners of the lit-up altar, two figures, or what, after a second, I decided must be figures, kneeling also. They were on either side of the empty praying stool in front of the altar, on which lay big gilt books and a couple of shimmering stoles. Lit up by that blaze of candles, their whitish folded robes looked almost like fluted marble columns; and as they knelt they ended off like broken columns, for they were, to all appearance, headless. Round their middle each had a white rope, about as thick as a hand, cutting the flutings of the robe; and where the head disappeared, a white penitent's hood thrown backward. They remained absolutely motionless, so that after awhile I began almost to doubt whether I had not interpreted some column or curtain into human figures. But after about five minutes one of the two—the right-hand one—moved slightly, just enough to show the thing was living. There they remained motionless, stooping in their fluted robes and thrown-back hoods, headless; and I went out, leaving them so, through the circular yard strewn with ivy and bay all round that worn away altar. What was it all? I have a vague notion this church is connected with the Cave of Cacus, or the lair of Romulus' she-wolf.

May 3

WINTER 1904

I

Palo

Palo again. The little pineta or grove rather of young pines, very close together and tufty, which open out and close fanlike in long green avenues, each with its prismatic star of shivering light, as we race through in the motor. A place where laurel-crowned poets in white should wander with verse-like monotony upon the soft green turf. Beyond, a band of lilac sere field, a band of blue sea; and between the fringe of the compact round pines, the sun setting, its light shivering diamond-like among the needles.

February 25

II

A Walk at Dusk

Yesterday went, in a band at dusk, for a melancholy stroll through the back streets. The Piranesi effect: yards of palaces, Marescotti, Massimo alle Colonne, the staircase of Palazzo Altieri. These immense grass-grown yards, with dreary closed windows all round, fountains alone breaking their silence, look like a bit of provincial life, of some tiny mountain town, enclosed in Rome. At Monte Giordano (Palazzo Gabbrielli) it becomes the walled Umbrian town, castellated. In this gloom, this sadness of icy evening sky between the high roofs, and after the appalling sadness of a church, squalid, dark, a few people kneeling, and the sacristan extinguishing the altars after a Benediction (every grief, one would think, laid down on that floor only to pick up a weight of the grief of others); after this there was something sweet and country-like in the splash of the fountains at Monte Giordano; the water bringing from the free mountains into this gloomy city; and to me the recollection of a Tuscan villa, of peace and serenity.

February 27

III

TUSCULUM

To Tusculum today with Maria and Du B. This is the place I carried away in my thoughts and wishes, a mere rapidly passed steep grassy hill, topped with pines and leafless chestnuts, from that motor drive last year round by Monte Compatri and Grottaferrata. The steepness and bareness of that great grass slope was heightened today by the tremendous gales blowing in a cloudless sky; one felt as if it were that wind which had kept the place so inaccessible, so virgin of trees and people, nay, had made the grass slippery, and polished the black basalt slabs of the path. And that wind struggling upwards against it in the sunshine, with the great rose and lilac sere hills opposite, the pale blond valley behind, seemed to clear the soul also of all rank vegetation, of all thoughts and feelings thick and muddy and leaden; to sweep away all that gets between the reality of things and oneself.

One should contrive to have impressions like these sufficiently often in life: this is the excitement which is helpful; the heartbeating, the breathlessness, the pain even, which brace and make us widely sensitive. Brother Wind—why did St. Francis not invoke him?—played with us roughly and healthfully, telling us, in the hurtling against houses, the rustling, soughing among trees, and the whistling in our own hair and ears, of the greatness of the universe's life and the greatness of our own.

On the crest, under the thin fringe of bare trees, with the plain of Rome, the snow of the Apennines on one side, the violet woods of Monte Laziale on the other, the surprise of suddenly coming on a rude stone cottage, with headless statues of athletes and togaed Romans built into its rough walls. And in a hollow under delicate leafless chestnuts that wonderful little theatre, cut out of black volcanic stone, as if the representation were to be storm and full moon, making and unmaking of mountains and countries, and the whole of history. . . Beginning to come down, and just above that little theatre, as we turned, we saw, beyond the dark ridge of Castel Gandolfo, cupolaed and towered, a narrow belt of light, more brilliant than that of the sky: the light upon the sea.

March 7

IV

St. Peter's

The greatness of the place had taken me, and quite unexpectedly, at once: the pale shimmer of the marble and the gold, the little encampment of yellow lights ever so far off close to the ground at the Confession; and, above all, the spaciousness, the vast airiness and emptiness, which seemed in a way to be rather a mode of myself than a quality of the place. I had come to see, if I could, Pollaiolo's tomb in the Chapel of the Sacrament. I found the grating closed; and kneeling before it, a foreign northern-looking man, with grizzled, curly hair and beard, and a torn fustian coat and immense nailed shoes. He was muttering prayers, kissing his rosary or medal at intervals, and slightly prostrating himself. But what struck me, and apparently others (for people approached and stared), was his extraordinary intentness and fervour. He was certainly conscious of no one and nothing save whatever his eyes were fixed upon—either the sacrament or the altar behind that railing, or merely some vision of his own. And he seemed not only different from everyone else, but separate, isolated from that vast place which made all the rest of us so small, such tiny details of itself. He was no detail, but an independent reality—he and his prayer, his belief, his nailed shoes: all come who knows how far in what loneliness! I got the sacristan to open, and went in to see the tomb—a mad masquerade thing, everything in wrong relief and showing the wrong side, the very virtues or sciences flat on their backs, so that you could not see them. And in the middle, presenting his stark bronze feet, the brown, mummied-looking, wicked pope, with great nose under his tiara. An insane thing—more so than any Bernini monument, I thought. Perhaps it was the presence of that man praying away outside which affected me to think this. There he was, as little likely to move away, apparently, as the bronze pope stretched out, soles protruded, among the absurd allegories. I went also to see the Pietà, and then stayed a long while walking up and down; but still the man was kneeling there, and might be kneeling, doubtless, till now or till doomsday, if the vergers had not, in closing the doors, turned him out.

March 8

VERNON LEE

V

THE CRYPTS

Yesterday the Grotte Vaticane, the Crypts of St. Peter's, a horrible disappointment, and on the whole absurd impression. That of being conducted (down a little staircase carpeted with stair cloth) through the basement of a colossal hotel, with all the electric light turned on at midday—a basement with lumber-rooms full of rather tawdry antiquities giving off its corridors, and other antiquities (as we see them in Italian inns) crammed against walls and into corners. Donatello and Mino bas-reliefs become sham by their surroundings, apocryphal Byzantine mosaics, second-rate pictures. Even empty sarcophagi and desecrated tombs just as at Riettis or Della Torres at Venice, and with seventeenth-century gilding and painting obbligato overhead. And then into wider corridors, whitewashed, always with that glare of electricity from the low roof; corridors where you expect automatic trucks of coals, or dinner lifts; and where the vague whitewashed cubes of masonry against the walls suggest new-fangled washing or heating apparatus. And instead! they are the resting-place of the Stuarts, only labels telling us so, or of mediæval popes. And that vague arched thing with wooden cover, painted to imitate porphyry, is the tomb of the Emperor Otho; and there, as we go on, it grows upon one that the carved and mitred figures tucked away under arches are not warehoused for sale to forestiere, but lying on the sarcophagus, over the bones or the *praecordia* of Boniface VIII of Roveres and Borgias.

Waiting at the head of that staircase for the beadle, faint strains of music come from very far. In St. Peter's a great choral service like this one going on in the left-hand chapel, becomes a detail lost as in the life of a whole city.

March 17

VI

SAN STEFANO

San Stefano Rotondo on that rainy afternoon, the extraordinary grandeur of this circular church filled with diffuse white light. Architecturally one of the most beautiful Roman churches, certainly, with its circle of columns surrounding the great central well, where two colossal pillars carry the triumphal arch, carry a great blank windowed wall above it, immensely high up. Those columns, that wall, pearly white, of carved and broken marble against pure chalky brilliancy of whitewash, seem in a way the presiding divinities of this great circular sanctuary in the church's centre; or is it the white light, the solemn pure emptiness among them? An immanent presence, greater certainly than could be any gigantic statue.

March 18

VII

Via Latina

Afterwards, in fitful rain, we went to the Tombs and the little roofless basilica near them in the Via Latina; and walked up and down, a melancholy little party enough, grubbing up marbles and picking them out of the rubbish heap among the quickening grass. The delicate grey sky kept dissolving in short showers; the corn and ploughed purple earth (*that compost!*) were drenched and fragrant with new life; and the air was full of the twitter of invisible larks. But in this warm soft renewal there was, for us, only the mood of lost things and imminent partings; and the song of the peasants in the field hard by told not, as it should, of their mountains, but of this sad, wet landscape traversed by endless lines of ruins. Suddenly in the clouds, a solid dark spot appeared; the top, the altar slab of Mons Latialis. And little by little the clouds slipped lower, the whole mountain range of hills stepped forth from the vapours, with its great peaceful life and strength.

March 18

SPRING 1905

I

Rome Again

Yesterday, after D. Laura's, took Du B. that walk through the Ghetto, along the Tiber quays by the island; a stormy, wet day. Rome again! As we stood by the worn Januses of the bridge and looked into the swirling water, thinking of how that Terme Apollo had lain there, the Tiber, like Marsyas, flaying one fair flank of the god; I felt Rome and its unchanging meaning grip me again, and liberate me from the frettings of my own past and present.

We went in to see some people who are furnishing an apartment in Palazzo Orsini. A very Roman impression this: the central court of that fortified palace built into the theatre of Marcellus; lemons spaliered and rows of Tangerine trees, with little Moorish-looking fountains between; only the sky above, only the sound of the bubbling fountains.

You look out of a window and behold, close by, the unspeakable rag-fair of that foul quarter, with its yells and cries rising up and stench of cheap cooking. We saw some small Renaissance closets, still with their ceilings and fire-places, where tradition says a last Savelli was stabbed. A feudal fortress this, and, like those of the hills round Rome which these ruins mimic, raising its gardens and pompous rooms above the squalor of the mediæval village. Immediately below, the corridors of the theatre; below that, the shops, where pack-saddles, ploughs, scythes, wooden pails—the things of a village—are for sale in the midst of those black arches. And then the dining-room, library, bath-rooms of excellent New Englanders crowning it all; and in the chapel, their telephone! "Take care," I said, "the message will come some day—not across space, but across time. *Con chi parlo?*" Well, say, *The White Devil of Italy!*

In that Campitelli quarter, the constant blind turnings behind the great giant palaces; places for cut-throats, for the sudden onslaught of bravos.

I feel very often that if one lived in all this picturesqueness, the horrors of the past, the vacuity of the present, would drive one I know not whither. I have had, more than ever this time, the sense of horror at the barbarism of Rome, of civilisation being encamped in all this human refuse, and doing nothing for it; and the feeling of horror at this absorbing Italy, and at one's liking it! They are impressions of the sort I had at Tangier. And the face of an idiot beggar—the odd, pleased smile above his filth—suddenly brought back to me that special feeling, I suppose of the East. We are wretched, transitional creatures to be so much moved by such things, by this dust-heap of time, and to be pacified in spirit by the sight of all this litter of ages; 'tis a Hamlet and the gravedigger's attitude; and the attitude of Whitman in the fertile field of *This Compost* is a deal better.

SABATO SANTO

Postscript

Yesterday morning, while looking through, with a view to copying out, my Roman notes of the last eighteen years, I felt, with odd vividness, the various myselfs who suffered and hoped while writing them. And, even more, I felt the presence of the beloved ones who, unmentioned, not even alluded to, had been present in those various successive Romes of mine. All of them have changed; some are dead, others were never really living. But while I turned over my note-books, there they were back. Back with their feeling of *then*; back with their presence (in one case the presence of a distant companion, to whom I could show these things only in thought); their complete realisation, or their half explicit charm, their still unshattered promise. Of all these I find not a word, barely a name; nothing telling of them to others. Only to me, in these sites, impersonal and almost eternal, on these walls which have stood two thousand years and may stand two thousand more, and these hillsides and roads full of the world's legend—there appear, visible, distinct, the shadows cast by my own life; the forms and faces of those changed, gone, dead ones; and my own.

Florence, *April*, 1905

A Note About the Author

Vernon Lee (1856–1935) was the pen name of Violet Paget, a British author of supernatural fiction. Born in France to British expatriate parents, Paget spent most of her life in continental Europe. A committed feminist and pacifist, she joined the Union of Democratic Control during the First World War to express her opposition to British militarism. A lesbian, Paget had relationships with Mary Robinson, Amy Levy, and Clementina Anstruther-Thomson throughout her life. Paget, a dedicated follower of Walter Pater's Aesthetic movement, lived for many years in Florence, where she gained a reputation as a leading scholar of the Italian Renaissance. In addition to her work in art history, Paget was a leading writer of short fiction featuring supernatural figures and themes. Among her best known works are *Hauntings* (1890), a collection of four chilling tales, and "Prince Alberic and the Snake Lady," a story which appeared in an 1895 issue of *The Yellow Book*, a controversial periodical that featured the works of Aubrey Beardsley, George Gissing, Henry James, and William Butler Yeats. Although Paget was largely forgotten by the mid-twentieth century, feminist scholars have rekindled attention in her pioneering work as a leading proponent of Aestheticism.

A Note from the Publisher

Spanning many genres, from non-fiction essays to literature classics to children's books and lyric poetry, Mint Edition books showcase the master works of our time in a modern new package. The text is freshly typeset, is clean and easy to read, and features a new note about the author in each volume. Many books also include exclusive new introductory material. Every book boasts a striking new cover, which makes it as appropriate for collecting as it is for gift giving. Mint Edition books are only printed when a reader orders them, so natural resources are not wasted. We're proud that our books are never manufactured in excess and exist only in the exact quantity they need to be read and enjoyed.

Discover more of your favorite classics with Bookfinity™.

- Track your reading with custom book lists.
- Get great book recommendations for your personalized Reader Type.
- Add reviews for your favorite books.
- AND MUCH MORE!

Visit **bookfinity.com** and take the fun Reader Type quiz to get started.

Enjoy our classic and modern companion pairings!

Bookfinity is a registered trademark of Ingram Book Group LLC. © 2023 Bookfinity. All rights reserved.

Printed in the USA
CPSIA information can be obtained
at www.ICGtesting.com
JSHW082356140824
68134JS00020B/2100